THE SOUND
OF A WRITER'S VOICE

THE SOUND
OF A WRITER'S VOICE
Both a Window and a Mirror

proving
press

Book Design & Production: Columbus Publishing Lab

www.ColumbusPublishingLab.com

Hardback ISBN: 978-978-1-63337-398-3

Paperback ISBN: 978-1-63337-397-6

E-Book ISBN: 978-1-63337-401-0

Printed in the United States of America

13 5 7 9 10 8 6 4 2

To hearts that yearn and minds that seek.

Flower in the crannied wall, I pluck you out of the crannies,
I hold you here, root and all, in my hand,
Little flower—but if I could understand
What you are, root and all, and all in all,
I should know what God and man is.

—Tennyson

If a man does not keep pace with his companions, perhaps it is because he hears a different drummer. Let him step to the music which he hears, however measured or far away.

—Thoreau

Foreword

Each piece of writing we consume as readers is, in some form or another, an expression of a writer's voice, a glimpse into his psyche, mindset, and ideals. Through the lens of his words he grants us permission to view the world briefly through his eyes.

The pieces contained within these pages are a truer representation of the author than you will find in most books. A compilation of thirty years of work, recorded by hand in a writing journal, Santiago's reflections are presented here raw and unedited, flowing in an intimate stream of consciousness from his heart to the page.

These entries are a chronological accumulation of mostly independent unities throughout the course of one life—personal observations, insights, commentary, reflections, and brief narratives. They voice our common struggle to find meaning and value in the great mystery that is life and the universe as we exist within it, both of which are full of wonder and violence and beauty on a scale that is hard to fathom.

The author has chosen to keep his true identity secret, and while you will not find his name printed here, you will find his identity as you read. The pseudonym "Santiago" may obscure the author from view in many ways, yet as you read, you will discover that he is starkly visible on every page.

It is the author's hope, and mine, that these writings will be a source of reflection for you, one that calls you back into yourself for introspection, for endless curiosity, and for peace.

I leave you with this note from the author:

> *If these pieces provoke, let them provoke in kindly ways; if they arouse, let them do so in ways that make you think and feel more keenly. Let them be little windows to look out of and little mirrors to look into. After all, I am not "other" to you, and you are not "other" to me.*
>
> *—Santiago*

May *The Sound of a Writer's Voice* help you in finding your own.

—Emily Hitchcock
CEO, Columbus Publishing Lab
May 27, 2020

I wish that you were here
To brave with me tonight this winter storm
That fills so full the space in front of me
With falling snow
I have to wince and squint
And even then can barely see
Just where it is I'm going,
Which is of little consequence to me, I guess,
Since where I'm bound this winter night
I do not know and little care,
And yet I have no need
To get completely lost
Or run headlong into a tree.
So thick and furious falls the snow
It almost frightens me,
But Oh, the wonder of it—
The pure ferocious beauty
That so beleaguers me
And buffets me about!
I scrunch my coat and scarf
More closely up around my neck
And push into the bleary wilderness
Of wind and snow,
Slogging through the cover on the ground,
Already ankle deep,
Plowing up a trail as I go.
I do not mean to mark the way I've come
And would regret the ragged trace
I leave behind
Except I know my tracks
Will be completely filled and smoothed

Continued

By blowing snow
Before I loose the laces of my boots.
It's good to be alone this winter night,
On such a tramp as this,
Yet all the same,
I wish I had you with me.

....

The caged bird
Sat on a wooden perch
And chirped what might have been a song
Except the notes had no wings
And dropped to the floor of the cage
And died among the newsprint
And the litter of cracked seeds
Near the conical pile of smudge
Caused by the bird choosing to sit
Almost entirely in one spot,
The one spot preferred
Because it was near the tin bell
And the cuttlebone
And the tiny looking glass.
The bird sat there,
Usually wondering
Why he was so beautiful
And what his wings were for
And why it was
The notes he made
Fell to the floor,
But today not thinking these things,
Sitting there instead,

Filled with anxiety,
Frozen in fear,
His heart
Beginning to beat out of control,
Glancing with terror
Out the side of one eye
At the door of the cage
Which had been left
Standing wide open.

....

When a lunatic came to his door
Frantically warning
That a wolf was loose in the woods
Larger than a cow
Devouring everything that moved,
The man picked up a walking stick
And whacked the fool over the head
And drove him away with a curse.
But that very night
The man boarded up his windows
And doubled barred the door
And slept with a pitchfork by his bed,
And in his sleep
He created a friendly fire-breathing dragon
To keep the horrible wolf
Out of his dreams.

It was late.
The sky was clear.
I stood over a puddle
Looking down into the sky
At the moon and stars.

....

In an old neglected cemetery,
Close to a rotting rail fence,
Hidden among the tall weeds,
Lie fragments from broken stone markers
Laid to rest in a ragged pile,
Some vandalized
By time and the elements,
Most by brave boys
Who do not know very much yet
About life and death.
On the broken piece of stone
At the bottom of the stack,
The chiseled side
Pressed firmly in the soft earth,
Providing a friendly habitat
For sow bugs and centipedes,
Are the remains of an epitaph
That human eyes
May never see again:

Sarah B.
Age 6
Gone, But Not Forgotten

The desert wayfarer
Staggered through the sand,
Near death,
His face scorched by the sun,
His lips cracked,
His eyes glazed,
When at length he came,
Astonishingly enough,
Upon a fountain
Bubbling up in the sand,
The water clear, cold, and sparkling.
He drank greedily
And plunged his face into it.
And soaked his hair,
And splashed it on his body,
Cooling it
And rinsing off the gritty sand,
Then, at last, refreshed,
He sighed contentedly
And continued on his way,
Unaware that an old lizard,
Lying in the shade of a nearby rock,
Had observed this bizarre pantomime
And was now studying the spot
Where the man had stopped,
Noting how a slight swirling breeze
Was lifting away the dust like particles
Of the disturbed sand.

When God was asked
By a young petitioner
If the human drama
Were a tragedy or a farce,
God broke into laughter
And laughed until he cried.

....

The King of all the Realm
Had fallen asleep in the grass
And was dreaming.
And in his dream
There was a nobleman
Who, oddly enough,
Was also asleep and dreaming.
And in the dream of the nobleman
A palace guard
Sat in the balcony of a theater
Watching a play,
And in the play,
Taking his bit part very seriously,
Was a small, very common, boy
Who was sitting
Slouched in a corner
Reading a book,
Set in a land of make believe,
About a most fantastic character
Who had fallen asleep in the grass
And was dreaming
That he was King of all the Realm.

"Do as I say,"
Said the great tiger
To the wild dog,
"Or I will tear you open
And feast on your heart."
"Tear me open then and eat,
Oh brave and mighty tiger,
But only if I do as you say,
Will you feast on my heart."

. . . .

He only is wise
Who learns there is no such thing
As the ugly truth,
And that evil
Is only good
We do not understand.

. . . .

She could have been
A tall Norwegian Spruce
Or any other mountain evergreen,
Growing free.
Instead, she is more like
A piece of topiary
Along a garden walk—
Or bonsai tree.

The thing I like best
About a bridge
Is that it doesn't really
Bring together;
It leaves the water in between
And can be blown up
At either end.

....

"There is but one test left,"
Said the master to the young pilgrim.
"I have a friend I want you to meet,"
Whereupon, a figure
Clothed in a long black robe
With a great hood pulled over the head
Entered the room,
Approached the young man,
And stood before him,
Silent and motionless.
The master then looked hard
Into the eyes of the youth and said,
"This is Death;
He is someone you should know."
The young pilgrim
Peered into the black void of the hood
And then without hesitation
Extended a hand
And said serenely,
"I am very pleased to meet you."
And a twinkle sparked in the master's eye,
And his face began to shine.

A child pulled an ugly rock
Out of the mud
And took it to the stream
And rinsed it clean
And carried it home in his hand.
That night he picked it up
And held it under the lamp:
"You are so beautiful,"
He said.
And placed the rock
On the stand
Beside his bed.
He had left the window open,
And when he woke in the morning
He found that the rock
Had flown away.

....

And there it was,
The Hammock of God,
Hanging limp and luminous
In a treeless forest
Located at the very heart of the black void,
Anchored at neither end,
The woven fabric
A continuous filament of white light.

"Why me?" he said,
Talking to the sky,
And he cursed
And kicked a rock
And broke his foot.

....

Which is harder—
To accept the stark fact
That you will someday die
Or to appreciate the stunning reality
That you are actually alive?

....

Have you ever felt
Like a butterfly
Wearing a straight-jacket
And kept in a box,
Or like a bald eagle
Chiseled out of stone?

....

Alone in the night
When the stars are still
And the wind is asleep in the trees,
I think of the time
We filled life's cup
And drank it down to the lees.

The suspicious man
Looked like the Prince,
Dressed as he was
In princely apparel.
But when the rebel inquisitors
Apprehended him
And removed the finery
They discovered
The man was wearing a burlap shirt
And soiled overalls,
That he was an impostor,
A peasant who had lost his wits,
And they cursed him
And drove him away.
Later that night
The Prince removed his burlap shirt
And fell asleep
With a smile on his face
And all his wit intact.

....

He inched through life
Bent over,
A heavy rope across his shoulder,
Dragging a great anchor
Which seemed to catch and snag
On every upturned rock and root,
Pushing before him
A rough cut block of black granite,
Whistling a merry tune
And sporting a twinkle in his eye.

A hungry desert snake
Emerged from beneath a rock
And slithered slowly
Through the sand in search of food.
As luck would have it,
He swam headlong into the path
Of a plump salamander
Which was filled with the holy spirit.
The snake,
Being familiar with lethal venoms,
Angled off at double time.

....

"Come," said the man,
"Are you prepared to face God
If Christ turns out to be
His only begotten son
And man's redeemer?"
"Let me answer that with a question,"
Came back the other:
"Are you prepared to face God
If it turns out that he was not?"

....

He had a special place
In the back corner
Of the bedroom closet,
Behind some boxes,
Where he would go
When he was lonely.

Sometimes
Without a thing to hold us down
We cannot rise,
Without a thing to bind us
We are not free,
Like a tree without roots
Or a kite without a string.

....

Reality is an illusion.

....

When a beautiful creature
Wandered into the land of the ugly,
The inhabitants fell upon
The hideous creature
And slew her.

....

What is a poet
But a kind of blacksmith
Who takes his heart
Out of the furnace,
Lays it on an anvil,
And beats it into words.

....

Where everyone is beautiful but one,
Only one is beautiful.

Man in the lighthouse,
Been there so long
He's lost his bearings.
Looking through the windows
He thinks he's the captain of a ship,
Lost at sea,
Standing on the bridge,
Looking for a light in the darkness.

....

"Master," beseeched a young inquisitor,
"Should a man live in the here and now,
Defined by the immediate,
The palpable,
The temporary,
Or should he,
Through imagination and intellect,
Haunt the far reaches of time and space
Contemplating the incomprehensible Cosmos?"
The Master was silent and still
For a long time.
Then he picked up a stick,
Drew a Spiral Galaxy in the loose dirt,
Slowly got to his feet,
And walked away,
Feeling the warmth of the Sun on his face
And holding a clump of periwinkle Violets
Under his nose.

What is true faith
But belief
Which has become so sheer,
So fused with certainty and expectation,
That doubt itself
Converts to the belief,
And all that is not possible
Explodes in possibility!

....

If you wear a mask too long
One of two things will happen:
Either the mask will slowly change
To fit your face,
Till at length it is no longer a mask,
Or your face will slowly change
To fit the mask
Till at length it is no longer your face.

....

When all men are equal, no man is free.

....

A man who believes only in the possible
Lives in a narrow cell
And wears a helmet made of lead.

If a silver bell cannot be struck
And made to shiver for a moment
In silver bliss,
It's just as well
That it were packed in cotton
And kept in a crate
And the crate kept
Locked in a hold of a ghostly ship
And the ghostly ship
Set free to drift forever
On the dark, unsilvered waters
Of a flat, unshivering sea.

....

When the others
Rejected and excluded him
Because he was different
And went off
Laughing and playing together,
He felt so awful
That he changed what was different about him
And became just like the others.
But when the others
Finally accepted and included him,
He felt even more awful than before,
And when they all romped off together,
Laughing,
He was not even vaguely aware
Why it was that deep down
He hated them.

A man sits alone in his chamber,
Miserable, disconsolate,
Beating his head with a stick,
Trying to drive out the certain knowledge
That he will one day die,
While out in the garden
Another man sits alone in wonder and awe,
Trying to comprehend and appreciate
The extraordinary fact
That he is actually alive!

....

He was not Miletus,
But an impostor.
However, he was such a good impostor
That many people
Began to confuse the two.
As time went on,
Miletus became increasingly uneasy,
And began to question his own identity
And soon was no longer convincing
As the genuine article.
And it was not long after that
That it was Miletus
Who appeared to be the counterfeit,
A pathetic impersonator,
And the impostor
Became the real Miletus.

They were legion.
Their bright flags snapped.
Their drums snarled and snared.
Ten thousand spears bristled.
A lone figure
Stood rigid and right
On his small piece
Of high ground,
Facing them,
His hand welded to his sword,
Wondering how he was going
To have strength enough
After the battle
To make ten thousand graves!

....

I watched in amazement
As a man,
Naked and unafraid,
Walked into the center
Of a great raging inferno
And stood there
Shuddering in savage pain,
But not crying out.
When after a few moments he emerged,
Blackened and seared inside,
I rushed to him,
Wincing in horror,
And asked him to explain
What he was doing.
He filled his lungs with air,

Expanding impressively,
Then puffed out his breath
In a sigh that was almost ferocious
And said,
"I am trying to make myself
Worthy of my dreams."

....

It was a perilous thing she was doing,
But she was determined
And would not be dissuaded.
"Why are you doing this dangerous thing?"
Asked a concerned observer:
"Are you not afraid?"
"Yes, I am afraid," she said.
"I am doing it
Because I am afraid."

....

Not in the confession of your sin,
But in the affirmation
Of your innocence,
Do I redeem you.
Not forgiveness,
But understanding I give;
Not mercy,
But acceptance.

One day a man came upon a Chaos,
And he was greatly disturbed
And could not bear the presence of it,
So he set to work with his tools
And built a frame around it
Which had a certain order
And balance
And proportion;
And he put a door in it
And windows with stained glass.
And when he was finished
He was at peace with himself
And called it Good.

....

How firm he stood,
How long he fought,
How much he bled,
How little difference he made,
And all for some stupid principle.
Surely he was a great fool.

....

A woman stood at the foot
Of a great, precipitous mountain,
Her head tilted up,
Her eyes,
Lofty and luminous,
Fixed on the summit.

On her shoulder
Hung a loose coil of rope,
Shoved under her belt
A small pick.
"Surely you're not thinking
Of climbing this mountain,"
Said an astonished observer.
But she gave no sign
That she had heard him,
And did not take her eyes
From the mountain top.
Then of a sudden,
She smiled:
"Do you see that tiny speck
There on the topmost pinnacle,
Waving at us in triumphant exaltation?
It's me," she answered
In a voice
That seemed to originate from far away
And to descend into his ears.

....

If you pretend
To be somebody you're not
And forget that you're only pretending,
You will have become what you aren't
And lost the chance
To be what you might have been
Which may be
No tragic loss to the world,
If you're an asshole by nature.

One man looked at another,
"You are a slave," he said.
The other,
Knowing no better,
Accepted the judgment of the one man
And spent his days
Dragging around a chain.
Then one day
He heard a voice from the sky:
"You are a noble Prince,"
Said the voice,
But knowing better
The slave only sighed
To hear such a cruel thing spoken.

....

If I attempted to count and appreciate
All the blessings in my life,
I would have no time
To count and appreciate
All the cursed people on this planet
Who have no blessings to count.

....

We should aspire
To live each hour of our life
Like the great red ruffled flower
Of the Hibiscus plant,
Which blooms in lavish splendor,
But only for a day.

Like the thunk of a tomahawk
Slamming into solid wood,
Or the almost soundless entry
Of a black sword
Into the very heart of Light,
Such is the sound of my loneliness.

....

If you're running away from something,
You're running the wrong way.

....

No finer words
Could chisel cut for him than these:
He stood his ground.

....

How did I feel when she died?
Like a vampire
When an iron stake
Is driven through its heart,
Or like a pair of eyes
When every light in the Cosmos
Is extinguished forever,
Or like God
When he wakes one morning
And finds mushrooms of light
Blossoming in his garden.

Because the thing in the Square
Was ugly and evil,
The mayor passed an ordinance
Forbidding the people
Ever to go near the thing,
Ever, ever, ever.
But when a few children
Whose curiosity
Exceeded their need to be obedient
Approached the thing
And were not struck dead,
They were emboldened.
And when they found
That the rats and snakes
And spiders and bats
Were all made of rubber,
And that the mud and slime
Could be scrapped and scrubbed away,
They went to work,
And soon it was clear
That the ugly, evil thing
Was beautiful and good.

....

The thing in the Square was ugly,
But when the town counselors
Covered it with flowers
And flooded it with colored lights
And surrounded it with soft music,
The people stopped
And swooned to look at it.

Master, What must I do to be saved?
My son,
There is no salvation of I
Unless it's this:
That you accept the gift of your life
As a glory in and of itself,
That is not less
Because it cannot last,
But more for that reason,
As new fallen snow is more,
And the silver sound
Of a struck bell.
Only when your gratitude and joy
That you ever lived at all
Obliterates your need to live forever
Will you know a glory
Greater than everlasting life.

....

The Darkness closes round
And rings me in.
I do not flinch
And make no sound of fear,
For I have been in love with Light
And cheered each day,
But I have also loved the night
And know that in the black of it
Is something Bright.

I am not obliged to love you
Simply because you are a member
Of the human race.
In fact,
Whenever in the company of human beings
 I post extra sentries around the vault
Where I keep my love.

....

"An animal is an animal,"
He lectured me.
"It cannot think, not like we do.
Sure, they can learn and remember things,
But it's merely simple conditioning.
They have no volition,
Hence no conscience,
Hence no immortal soul.
Has an animal ever martyred itself
Or been convicted of first degree murder?
Have you ever seen an animal
On its knees
Sobbing uncontrollably,
Confessing its sins?
I rest my case."

....

I don't know quite how to speak of her.
In my dark night
She was to me
A soft light, a glow,

That let me know
The darkness in my heart
Was not complete.
In my sad silence
She was to me a Silver sound
That found its way into my stillness
And turned my stillness into Song.
What more is there to say:
As if in answer to a desperate prayer,
When most I needed someone,
She was there.

....

God said to the man before him,
"Say the two words
That will gladden my heart."
"Forgive me?"
"No," said God:
"Thank you."

....

They rejected him because he tied
A red bandana over his hair
And wore a silver ring
In one side of his nose,
Which is to say,
They rejected him
Because he rejected them.

This wondrous, wretched night,
This late and lonely hour,
I sit here all alone
And more alone
Than I have ever been,
Reborn inside,
But ruined,
Made whole only to be cut in half
And bleeding now
As I have never bled before.
And what of you?
Can you be bearing up
And holding onto life
When I am barely keeping death at bay?
I pray that angels keep you safe
While demons
Make cruel sport of me.

....

He was a good Christian,
A true believer,
Sure of his place in paradise,
But when one day
While he was walking alone
In the woods
He saw a shimmering curtain
Of fine iridescent light
Appear between two trees,
He stopped
And was filled with wonder and dismay;
And when the figure of Christ,

Clothed in a white cotton robe,
Emerged from the curtain,
As from another dimension,
And beckoned the man to follow him,
The color ran from the face
Of the true believer,
And he fled from the Presence
Like an arrow
Loosed from a mighty bow—
Or a clown
Shot out of a cannon.

....

Ugliness is just a word we use
To describe that part of the whole
Which we cannot understand
And do not approve,
But the whole would not be beautiful
Without the ugly parts.

....

Tell me what you remember,
And I will tell you who you are.

....

Only a few asylums exist
On the planet of the happy and carefree,
Erected there to tend to the needs
Of those who take themselves seriously.

"Be yourself,"
Is good advice
If you know who you are
And you are not a fanged thing,
Lurking in the dark,
Thirsting for blood.

....

We are fictitious characters
Who suffer from the delusion
That we are real;
We are phantoms
Strutting about impressively
As if we had form and substance,
Like creatures sculpture of smoke
Who have this notion
They are cast in bronze or stone.

....

What is the difference
Between the thoroughgoing determinist
Who believes
He is the predictable consequence
Of the unerring law of cause and effect
And the true believer
Who accepts predestination
And has surrendered
Body and soul
To the will of God?

Regaining consciousness,
He became aware first
Of the pain his hands,
Which felt as if they were on fire
Or had been thrust into boiling water;
Then of the unsteady yellow light
That played off the stone walls
And seemed to flutter about
Like drowsy moths;
Then of the calm presence
Of a woman who sat near him
And spoke soft words
Of comfort and hope
And placed a damp cloth
On his forehead.
Lying there in the near dark
Watching the wobbly light,
Pierced by the pain
In his hands and feet,
Miraculously alive,
He let his eyes fall closed
And moaned,
"My God, my God.
Forgive my doubt:
Thou hast not forsaken me."

....

Beware all sticky webs,
For where the web is hung
Nearby the spider lurks.

If we would better understand
Our human nature,
We would do well to consider
The nature and dynamics
Of the Wild Kingdom,
Out of which we fought our way
And of which we are still apart.

....

He navigated down his road,
Fixed in his ways,
Firm his beliefs,
Lost, deluded,
Casually,
Almost unconsciously,
But deftly,
Managing sidestep
Every stumbling block of Truth
In his way.

....

Fear? One fear only I have,
That the great temptation
Will catch me off guard someday,
And in a moment of weakness
I will fall to my knees
And beat my breast
And surrender my fierce spirit
To become a lamb of God.

Once he was young,
And his heart was an unbroken colt.

....

"Do you believe in God," he asked,
As if to hem me in
With this one pointed spear.
"I believe in the Cosmos,
Ever changing,
That cannot be explained
More than to say in some form
It always was and always will be;
That it is vast,
Beyond our ability to imagine,
And mysterious and magical
Beyond our power to understand.
The Cosmos is not possible,
Yet the galaxies turn
And the stars glint and sparkle
And you and I,
Intelligent,
Inquisitive creatures,
Sit here, confounded,
Conscious of it and of ourselves,
Ourselves impossible.
Perhaps the Cosmic Stuff itself
Is all the God there is—
And God enough.

Every once in awhile
I get this faint but certain feeling
That somewhere deep in my being,
Buried alive
Beneath the weight of many years,
There dwells still
A happy little boy
Who lived in wonder
And in trees,
And dreamed and dared
And did stupendous things,
And all but blazed with life,
Who could not see beyond today
And had no vision of himself
As ever grown up.
I wonder what
That little boy would think
To see the man he has become.
Perhaps the man he might have been
Is buried there beside the boy
He used to be;
Perhaps that is why
The faint but certain feeling
Seems shot with something sad.

....

She had been abducted,
Raped,
And brutally murdered.
They found her T-shirt
Caught in a bush

Where it had been tossed aside
During the spate
Of obscene violence.
It was smudged
And torn
And stained with blood.
And when the police lieutenant
Held it before him in his fingertips,
Carefully pinched at the shoulders,
And read the words
That were beautifully scripted
In soft colors,
He felt as if
He had been struck in the chest
With a great axe:
"Practice Random Kindness
And Senseless Acts of Beauty."

....

God looked with disappointment
At the man who stood before him,
And when the man saw
That God was not pleased,
He fell to his knees,
Trembling,
And whimpered,
"What can be wrong?
All my life I always did
Exactly what I was supposed to."

The word soul
Is a long supple stick
Which people with athletic egos
Use to vault themselves
To everlasting life.

....

Who is my hero?
You mean next to the Amazing Randy?
Well, in the little town of Circleville,
At the intersection of the two main streets,
Looms a large old brick building
Which used to be the armory
But is now a quiet fortress for books;
And both sides of the long sloping slate roof
Of that brick building
Reach up maybe four stories high
And come together making a long, impressive ridge,
And on that ridge,
Sitting stout and straight and fierce
And full of hungry vigilance,
Is a large phony owl,
A counterfeited menace
Put there to intimidate the local pigeons.
Driving by that old brick building the other day,
I noticed with a little amusement
And a great deal of admiration
That fifteen or twenty pigeons
Were roosting comfortably on the ridge,
Some sitting so close to that old scare owl
That you might speculate

They felt a little safer there.
Next to the Amazing Randy
My hero is the first pigeon
That noticed the stationary predator never moved,
Not ever, not even to breath or blink,
And wondered why,
Then flew near and circled his fear
And then, finally,
With trembling courage,
Made a clumsy landing on the roof.

....

And when the true believers,
The lambs of God,
Came upon the wolf
Who howled through the cold lonely nights
In disbelief,
They fell upon the heretic
And smothered him
In their soft warm wool.

....

You have heard it observed,
"Except ye see signs and wonders
Ye will not believe,"
But I say to you,
Beware,
Especially when you see signs and wonders.
Hasten then to doubt.

What do you mean I must have faith?
I do have faith, great faith—
In Reason.

....

"Hopelessly neurotic,"
Said the therapist to a student
As they observed
The hectic and repetitive behavior
Of the agitated case mouse.
"How was his neurosis caused?"
Asked the student?
"Well, it's a classic case,"
Began the therapist.
"The poor fellow
Spent all his adult life
In a small cage,
Every day running the wheel till exhaustion,
Then forced to sleep on a grid
Through which at periodic intervals
Was sent a mild but aversive current."
"Ah," said the student;
"It is no wonder then."
"Oh no, you misunderstand,"
Returned the teacher.
"You see, his neurotic symptoms
Did not appear
Until he was removed from the apparatus."

A man confined himself alone in a room
With the creature of his belief,
And smote the creature with a solid stick
And hurled great stones at it
And stabbed it again and again
With a sharp knife
And doused the creature with scalding water
And tried to smother it.
"But why do you abuse your belief
In such a savage manner," asked one
Who witnessed the brutal attack;
"You will surely kill the gentle creature."
"Beliefs are not gentle, my friend,"
Replied the man:
"They are ferocious predators.
I am trying to kill my belief
Because only if I cannot
Can I truly believe.
I will not stake my life
By something I can kill."

....

I felt sorry for the poor fellow,
Shuffling along,
Sweeping the ground with his stick,
Feeling his way.
"How was it that you lost your eyes," I asked.
"I'm sorry, Sir, but you are mistaken;
I walk in glorious Light.
It's you who can see
That is fumbling along in the dark."

I knocked the frozen wood
Against a rock to jolt away
The snow and ice.
The hard wood rang
And nearly ruined my hand
And sent a shock inside
That rattled bones
And caused my brain to flinch.
The knock shook loose the heavy snow,
But still the wood maintained a frosty look
And no amount of pounding
Could jar away the bits of gravely ice.
I brought an armful in
And stood the pieces on the hearth
Near the black box stove
Which soon would hiss and crackle hot,
But now stood cold and still,
Like something dead there on my hearth.
An hour later it must have been
When I returned with kitchen match and kindling
And set about to make a fire.
I kneeled down
And looked with wonder at the wood
That stood there crusted over still
With snow and patchy ice.
The house was warm enough
Without a fire in the stove
To melt away the winter blight upon the wood,
But there it was
Just as it was an hour ago.
And then it came to me:

The wood was frozen to the core,
To the heart wood.
The cold inside, the deep cold,
Held off the thaw.
"I've known people like this," I thought,
And quickly put aside the possibility
That I was one of them.
I turned then to the stove.
I raised the latch
And swung the hinged door out,
Then looked inside
To see if any bits of wood were left unburned.
Sometimes the fire dies
While there is yet life left
Lingering in the last to burn.
I saw the fire's work had been complete—
The little crematory was good at what it did—
And took my rake
And worked to level out the wood's remains.
When suddenly my arm was seized by wonder
And my whole being stopped to stare,
For there among the dusty death of wood,
There in the powdered ash,
Buried alive two days ago,
A glowing ember lay.
I marveled at it
Then turned to marvel once again
The ice upon the standing wood.

And when the man
Had done what God had told him not to do,
There kindled in God's eye
A spark that danced a jig
And romped about without restraint,
And the mouth of God began to stretch
And spread across His face.

. . . .

Let your beliefs—
Let even what you know—
Be modeled in clay that will not harden
With hands that won't be still.

. . . .

A hundred times,
A hundred thousand times better it is,
To squirm in pain
On a bed of sharp, authentic nails
Than to slumber drowsily
On a couch
Upholstered out of wishful thinking.

. . . .

Your hunger to know
Should never give you
An appetite to believe.

"If I could see
Maybe I would believe," she said.
"If you could believe
Maybe you would see," tutored another.
"I do not want to pay
That high a price for sight.
Better to be blind
Than see what isn't there," she answered back.
"Perhaps you're right," the other said,
"But is it not possible to be blinded also
By what you see?"

....

I do not do what I do
Because it is right.
What I do is right
Because I am doing it.

....

It is not possible to commit suicide;
It is an act
Of pinching the wick of a candle
Which is already charred and cold.
A man takes his own life
Only after he has been murdered.

Two women sat grieving.
"Why are you so downcast and desolate?"
Asked one of the other.
"I grieve because I have lived with abandon.
My life has been a self-indulgent binge,
But I am sated now,
And now the small sharp teeth of guilt
Gnaw at me,
For I feel I have wasted my life
And lived in vain.
You see, I was a passionate woman
And my heart flamed
And finally burned to ashes.
And you,
Why do you sit under such a dark cloud?"
"I grieve because I've lived a life
Of self restraint;
Always I denied myself
And sacrificed for others.
I was a true altruist,
A paragon of virtue—
Some even thought me a saint.
But now the claws of deep regret
Tear at me,
For my heart smothered to death
And molders in my breast,
For I too was a passionate woman.

So you've had a religious experience, have you?
That tells me only this:
That you found yourself
Incarcerated in reality
And were unhappy and escaped,
And that now you are safely and happily
Incarcerated elsewhere.

....

Come, my son,
Speak your mind freely
And do not be afraid.
We are understanding and tolerant
And respect those who disagree with us.
We will open our minds
And listen patiently
And do everything in our power
To show you why
You are wrong.

....

What he was planning to do was crazy.
It would ruin him.
He was out of control.
Surely he was mad.
But he came to his senses just in time
And lived the rest of his life
In a straight-jacket.

A beautiful gray fox
Sat motionless on a log
That lay angled across a stream,
His eyes filled with light,
His heart shot with joy.
Sitting there alone and still
He looked as if he'd somehow made one
With the sight and sound
Of all that he could see and hear,
And with the scent
Of all that he could smell,
And with the sensations
Of all that he could feel:
And because of that,
It appeared to me
That he had been beatified,
That he was in the blessed state,
Even though
He could not tell you right from wrong
And never talked with God.

....

He had freed himself
From the petty tyranny
Of right and wrong,
And therefore never judged
Nor saw injustice done.

The solitary dweller
Who lived in the deep woods
Was so menaced by a ferocious beast
That whenever he left his dwelling
He had to arm himself with stones
And carry a stout spear.
Over and over again
He was attacked
And forced to do battle
With the fierce creature,
But always,
Though only with great exertion,
He prevailed
And drove the shrieking beast
Back into the density
Of the dark forest.
But when the rapacious thing
Finally had had enough
And did not return to menace him,
The solitary dweller
Soon became uneasy and restless,
And it was not long after that,
To his own dismay,
That he found himself
Leaving near his dwelling
And on his common paths
Pieces of raw meat.

The Moon steps out
Behind the clouds.
How lovely and romantic
The cold, lifeless thing is.

....

The box stove in my den rumbled inside
As hungry flames
Growled and gnawed on seasoned wood.
As I sat there
Feeling the radiant energy on my face
I watched with utter amazement
As a tiny man crawled out
The small, wedge-shaped opening
Which was the only way out of the inferno.
He could not have been
More than two inches tall
And was wearing,
Of all things,
A tiny black tuxedo
And a shiny top hat.
With one hand he brushed the ashes
Off the front of his pants
And the lapels of his coat.
From the other hand
Dangled a wee violin and a bow.
He then sat down
On the narrow ledge of the stove,
Crossed his legs,
Carefully placed the violin under his chin,
Positioned the bow,

And began to play with magnificent virtuosity
A Bach concerto.
Is this a fantastic tale?
Multiply the temperature inside the stove
A hundred million times
And have it take
Near fifteen billion years
For the virtuoso
To crawl out of the wedge,
And I tell you it is true.

....

One man sees a beggar.
He feels sorry for him.
He helps him to his feet,
Secures for him a night's lodging,
And gives him enough money for a hearty meal.
Another man sees a beggar.
He does not feel sorry for him.
But he believes he ought to help the man,
So he takes him by the arm,
Walks him to an inn
And secures for him a night's room and board.
Both men have been equally charitable.
Is one more deserving praise?
Which?

He did not obey like the others.
He seemed to have no desire to conform,
No need to be accepted,
No ability to subordinate his own puny ego
To the Great Society.
We served him
As we serve all others,
But he refused to sacrifice part of himself
To the Common Good.
He did not want our services, he said.
He said he would prefer to serve himself
And be left alone.
He did not have to believe;
Only to comply,
But he would not.
He was a selfish misfit
And a menace to the General Welfare.
He even delighted
In thinking of himself as an individual.
So in the name of Social Harmony
And Social Justice,
We killed him,
And it made us glad
To do something so beneficial
For the Colony of Man.

....

I am sitting here watching a movie
Recorded on a video tape.
I don't know what will happen next
But the tape knows.

Maybe life is like that.
Maybe we are all on a tape
And what will happen to us—
And to the mayfly
And to the milky way—
In a very real sense
Already has!

....

Once upon a solitary desert walk
I came upon a spiteful scorpion,
Stalking about,
Carrying his tail high,
Ready to strike out
At any hapless creature he came upon.
"Why do you prance about so aggressively?" I asked,
Gingerly keeping my distance.
"What has made you so mean and vindictive?"
"One time," hissed the scorpion,
"I was a human being like you,
And I lived my life
Repressing all hostility,
Believing that it was ennobling
To endure injustice
And that undeserved suffering was redemptive.
At the moment of my death
I was reincarnated out of what I had become,
Or should I say
Into what I had become."

What you believe
Is fantastic and incredible
What faith you must have
To believe things
Almost impossible oven to imagine.
Does your religion have a name?
Yes. We call it Science.

....

We talk a good sermon
On the value of the individual,
Of being different,
Of going against the grain,
Of standing alone;
But nearly every time
A true individual emerges,
It gives us a peculiar sense of satisfaction
To crush the radical.

....

He always obeyed the law
And always,
Though sometimes grudgingly,
Did what he was supposed to.
He resisted temptation
And held himself
To the highest standards of moral conduct,
So when an executioner was needed
He competed ferociously for the job.

I watch a little yellow wind-up toy
Wobble rigidly about
On the hardwood floor,
Moving with erratic precision
As if in keeping with a mindless plan,
A strutting little mechanism
Clicking and grinding out its life
In periodic motion,
Its ultimate purpose
To amuse a young child—
Or an idle god.

....

Tightly bound to a pole,
A woman slumped against the bindings
That kept her nearly erect,
Vaguely aware
Of an endless queue of people
That filed past her.
Some hurling insults and imprecations,
Some stones,
People who glared and cursed and spat.
"What awful thing did she do?"
Asked a horrified witness
Of one standing near the scene.
"She committed the great sacrilege,"
The other replied:
"She had the unmitigated audacity
To question the Truth."

"He was so just and conscientious,"
Noted one who knew him well.
"How did it happen?"
"It's a sad, cruel story," replied another.
"You see, when he saw a drunken brute
Abusing a poor woman on the street,
He interfered,
And the brute naturally took offense—
In fact was morally outraged—
And saying, 'Who made you God,'
Raised a great cudgel
And dashed out his brains."

....

What do you mean
I'm not being honest with myself,
I'm living a lie?
It's not true.
I'm the most authentic person I know.
The artificially, the phoniness,
Is genuine.

....

What was the lesson of the Holocaust:
That the heart of man
Is darker than we thought
And the heart of God
Must have been forged,
As a document can be forged—
Or a piece of iron.

When I see hatred and violence
And have my heart break and bleed,
Yet see no evil done;
When I see love and tenderness
And have my heart
Made warm and whole,
Yet see no good;
Then have I achieved
The blessed state.

....

Those who feel
They are separated from God
Have not yet been completely born,
Like tadpoles
Or caterpillars;
Or have not yet been put to vital use,
Like a whistle
Carved from a hollow reed
That has not felt the touch of lips
Or known the rush of wind,
Or a bell made out of silver
That has not yet
Been lifted up and shook.

....

We lost our land
And our liberty
And our way of life,
But we kept the peace.

The clown was a sight—
Mop hair, round, red nose,
Face a careful work of grease-paint art,
And what a repertoire of foolish stunts
And harmless falls
And funny pranks.
But the fact is
The mop hair
And the round red nose
Were his,
Were real,
And his face was not painted at all,
And he behaved quite naturally
And was not redeemed by the laughter.

....

The ancient woman
Was so bent over,
Her back so humped by bone disease,
She had not seen the moon
For many years
And could not lift her face enough
To look you in the eye.
And it is sadder still to tell
That there is not one left in all the world
To remember that glorious day
Eighty years ago
When she pulled on her cheerleading sweater
For the first time.

I turned out the lights
And knelt beside my daughter's bed,
Which is the only place I kneel,
And when I bent
To leave a kiss upon her cheek
And she looked up at me,
I saw reflected in her eye
A tiny luminescent moon
Lounging in the eastern sky
And looking through her window.
I stopped for a moment
To gaze and marvel at
The bit of errant sunlight
That at that most unlikely hour,
Blocked by the earth,
Yet found through night
A most delightful way
Into my eye.

....

Not literally, of course,
But still in a coarse way,
We are cannibals at heart,
Some of us;
In fact,
It is upon the heart
That we most often feed,
Many times on other hearts—
More often on our own.

There was in the woods I walk,
Far off any path,
Too deep among the other trees
By any walking on a path to see,
A great old oak.
I found it one day, when,
Disillusioned with the ways of men,
I left the trail
And pushed into the forest
At the densest place that I could find,
Perhaps to find some solace
In the ways of trees.
I fought my way
Through briared undergrowth,
Which fought back
And gave a good account of itself,
And almost had me once,
Until at length I extracted myself
And found that I was standing upright
In a small clearing.
And in the center of the clearing,
Stood the straight and massive trunk
Of the Great Oak.
What a thing of strength and beauty
To come on when I was weak
And out of love with life!
I slowly made my way to it
And pressed my length against it
And held full half its girth
In my extended arms,
And almost instantly

Was strong and brave and true again.
Over the years,
When spirits sagged and heart grew weary,
I fought my way to that great tree,
Which was my brother
And my father
And my friend
And the nearest thing to God
I've ever known.
The briars were especially cruel the day
I found it broken on the ground.

....

Two things equally beautiful,
Equally good.
Equally true:
Five blue robin eggs
Clustered in the bottom of a nest
In close to the trunk
Of a small Norwegian spruce,
Lying beneath the mother's warm breast,
A bit of biomagic taking place
Inside each one;
A fat possum
Under the cover of night,
Waddling away from a small Norwegian spruce,
Dragging a scaly cord like tail,
Still licking the gooey biomagic
From its pointed snout.

When will I know that I am truly wise?
When I can walk through a grove
Of flowering crabapple trees in early May
And be not in Heaven,
And lean against barbed wire at Auschwitz
And watch an Exodus of smoke
Black the morning sky
And be not in hell.
But what am I
When I am truly wise?
Wonderless and blankly contemplative
As a rock
Or a "God"

. . . .

"But if you break ranks
And try to leave the holy procession
We will have no choice
But to fall upon you
And slay you,"
Warned one of the men
Carrying a sacred baton.
"I choose to leave for that very reason."
"You mean you want to be slain?"
"I mean I do not choose to stay
With those who would slay me
If I chose to leave."

"We have the right and the power
To impose the peace," said the general,
"And there will be peace,
Even if we have to make it and keep it
With violence and bloodshed."

....

The old man sat so still,
There at the meadow's edge,
His back against a tree,
That you might think
Some wizard put a spell on him
And turned him into stone.
And if you saw the yellow finch
Wobbling on the stem
Of the corncob pipe
He had clamped between his teeth
And bobbing seed out of the bowl,
You'd have to blink away the disbelief,
But there he sat,
And there,
With the old man's breath on his tail,
Stood the wild bird and ate.
I wonder if the craft of meditation
Works this way,
And if a man sat quiet enough
And still enough
And long enough
He might attract a wild God.

A man of considerable position and responsibility,
Sitting on a bench in a tailored suit,
Buttons on the collar of his shirt,
Sharp creases in his pants,
Polish on his shoes,
His briefcase on the ground between his legs,
Waiting for a bus,
Turns to look directly at the derelict
Slumped over beside him on the bench,
Huddled in a mess of soiled clothing,
A melancholy weariness in his faded blue eyes.
Several times in recent weeks
They had seen and taken note of each other,
But neither one had made a move to speak.
But now,
Prompted by a more or less genuine sympathy
For the poor soul
And by the nagging thought
That maybe this was Jesus in disguise,
Posing here to test him,
The man of considerable position and responsibility
Said softly and compassionately,
"Pardon me.
I don't mean to interfere.
But is there anything
That I could do for you?"
The weathered brown face angled toward him
And a bit of morning light
Freshened the blue of his eyes,
And there was absolutely
No sarcasm or insincerity in his voice

When he responded,
With equal softness and compassion,
"It's funny you should ask me that;
I was about to ask you the same thing."

....

How will we know the carnivores
When we see them?
They will be the vegetarians.

....

Two men
Standing in the company of two plants:
"I wonder if they have consciousness,
As we have—
You know,
If they are really aware,
Really think and feel things."
"I don't think so,"
Replied the other plant.

....

I sat with the master this morning
And listened to him for an hour
And left more balanced and composed,
More centered in the Cosmos.
"What did he say?"
He did not speak a word.

There are some men
Loose in the world today who,
If they had before them
A doomsday button they could push
Which would exterminate
The race of man,
Would not,
In their extremity,
Hesitate to push it.
There are times
When I think I am one of those men.
Yet I would sacrifice a thousand galaxies
To hazard into life
A single contemplative mind.

....

Two men approached
Walking very slowly.
I heard the one coaching the other:
"Don't let it bother you.
Just ignore it.
There's nothing you can do,
So put it out of your mind.
Don't give it power over you."
As the two men passed,
I noticed it was not the man talking
Who had the surly scorpion
Perched on the collar of his shirt.

The tree,
Which might have boldly stretched
Into the upper blue
And etched a mark in the sky,
Stands cropped and cramped
Beneath the power lines.
How many such people I know.

....

When asked about his hate
He leveled me with this:
I could not hate
With such passion now
Had I not once
With equal passion loved.

....

She sat there alone,
Unconscious of herself
But seeming conscious of all else.
"Who is she?" I asked.
"No one knows.
Several of us have asked her name,
But she just looks through us
And smiles unknowingly
And says, 'I have forgotten.'"

It seemed to me I was asleep and dreaming,
And in my dream I was writing a poem,
But I dozed off while I was writing it
And dreamed again
That I was writing a poem.
Then I awoke from that dream
And found in my lap
The piece of writing I had dreamed about,
And I was sure then
That I had not been dreaming after all.
And then I woke again
And could not find the poem.
So now I figure I am wide awake
And writing this account,
But it could be that I am still asleep
And writing in a dream,
But if I am,
And you are reading this,
Well—

....

So clear the night sky!
So bright the points
Of crystal light
That prick my eyes
And make of my black-heavened heart
A glinting firmament!

"You mean you would break away from the others
Just for the sake of breaking away,
And for no other reason,
Just to be contrary,
Just to be different?"
"Yes."

....

When she took off her mask
And showed us what she really looked like,
We admired her for having the courage
To reveal herself to us.
And we thought she was truly beautiful,
And it did not occur to us
That she was wearing a mask
Beneath her mask,
And I don't think
That it occurred to her.

....

A random act
Is simply a predictable event
Which we cannot predict,
A perfect consequence
Of antecedents
Too complex for us to understand.

I am tired of hearing
From the weeping evangelicals
About how much Jesus suffered,
About the agony he endured,
The innocent lamb led to slaughter.
He was a beautiful revolutionary man, Jesus,
And he had a grim three days
There at the end,
And he suffered and died
With courage and dignity,
But I can think of many
Innocent lambs
Who suffered so much more,
Unspeakably so much more,
Sala Paulawitz for one,
And six million others
Come immediately to mind.
"Yes, but the difference there
Is that Jesus chose to die,"
The preacher will hurry to explain.
"He could have saved himself
But he chose to suffer for us
And to die in our stead."
And I would reply that
While dying is the ultimate price
A person can pay
For standing up for his beliefs,
It is a price many have paid,
And then I would ask him this:
Suppose God revealed himself to you,
Or to any one of us,

And told you
That you were his only begotten son
And that He had chosen you
For a special mission
Which would redeem all humankind
From certain and everlasting damnation
And made it clear that at the end
You would be betrayed, arrested,
Condemned, scourged, and crucified,
But if you chose to sacrifice yourself
You would not only please Him,
But would propitiate the sins of the world,
And after the ordeal was over
You would be resurrected
And ascend into Heaven to be with Him.
Would you do it?
I don't want to minimize
The martyrdom of Jesus,
But only an abject coward
Or a brazen fool
Or an intellectual,
Under those conditions,
Would turn God down.

The disguise she wore
Was quite convincing,
So convincing in fact
That when she was not incognito
She didn't recognize herself.

Of all the gods
That I have never really known,
None appeals more to my inner sight
Than Bright warm mother Sun.
I think the ancient worshippers
Got as close to getting it right
As anyone.
In all the vast expanse
Of cold and dark,
God is Light!

....

I hold in my hand,
Moments ago alive,
Just before the thunk
On the plate glass window,
The small soft corpse
Of the beautiful indigo bunting,
Still warm,
Still seeming so alive,
So lovely still.
"I'd trade my life right now,"
I thought,
"To see her breast expand again,
To see this fallen angel thing
Shudder back to life
And then explode again
In wild flight!"

Sometimes there is in me
A Brightness so exquisite Bright
That every fiber of my being
For a time
Is blinded into bliss,
And for a time,
My heart and soul
Could power stars
And splatter joyful light
All over every dark and dismal thing,
And for a moment
I am almost sure
The vast and starry Kingdom
Has a King!

. . . .

The ruffled peonies
Are much too soft
And fresh
And white
And full of devastating scent
For me to bear
This early day in June,
Sitting here,
At close of day,
Alone
And loveless as a brick.

The vicious woman,
Full of hate,
Was once a lovely girl
Desperate for love

....

He threw a knife at me
That stuck in my chest,
And when I winced
And cried out in pain
And looked at him accusingly,
He said.
"Hey, don't look at me
As if it's my fault.
You should have ducked out of the way.
It's time you started accepting responsibility
For your own pain.
You're not going to lay
The guilt on me."
And he stalked off indignantly,
Leaving me alone with my pain—
And his guilt.

....

Death is not only
The price that things alive
Must ultimately pay;
Even dead things
Will one day die,
The days of Sun and Moon and Earth

Are as precisely numbered
As the days of men.
Even the vast and mighty Milky Way
Will age at last
And keep a rendezvous
With some far off but final day.
Death is not
For only things alive.
And yet I know
That things alive,
And all celestial things,
Are not from dust to dust,
As some believe,
Are not from night to night,
But move from Fire to Fire,
From Light to Light,
And in that magic motion
You and I
And all substantial things
Have our state
Of evanescent Being.

....

To one alone in the woods,
Deep into night,
Unable to sleep,
A forest mouse
Nosing about in dry leaves
Can sound for all the world
Like a wild boar
Or grizzly bear.

I'm still a hound
And out there still
In the briars and the backwoods
Of Galactic Wilderness,
Still on the trail of God,
But is my muzzle
Really to the ground,
And am I powered by the scent
Of what I hunt?
Or am I on the run,
And splashing into streams
And boring through
The thickest undergrowth
That I can find
To keep from being hunted down?

....

The evening sky,
With puffs and streaks and swirls
Of white and blue
And pink and gray,
Will never ever be again
As it is now,
And even now is fading fast away,
But should I grieve
That such a present splendor
Will not keep?
Should I despair
That I was ever wide awake
Because so soon
I will forever sleep?

I hear this early hour
The far off cooing
Of the mourning dove,
Such a softly melancholy sound,
A little like the sound
We used to make as boys,
Blowing through our thumbs
Into the hollow of our hands,
So glad of life then,
The sound then
Not a plaintive coo
Or solemn knell,
But more a vital, sounding call
As from a battle horn
Or some enchanted shell.

....

The midday sky
Was bright and burnished blue,
And I,
Pretending it was night,
Looked into it
With special sight
At all the stars
I could not see.

....

Woe to bird with eagle heart
And wings of stone.

An old fisherman
Sits alone in a rowboat
In the middle of the loch,
Looking from the bank
A little like a lotus flower,
His heart still large and muscular,
But his old hands
Not what they used to be.
He has them
Lashed securely to the pole
Against the chance
His strength should fail him
When finally the strike is made.
He waits with patient resolution
As he has done for over sixty years,
Hoping to hook the monster of the loch,
Knowing it will take him
Down with it into the deep,
But unafraid to venture there
Where he has always fished.

....

She was fierce and defiant,
And took such wicked joy
In my distress.
I've never seen one
Filled with such sublime contempt.
Her hatred of me
Seemed almost exquisite.
It must have been
That once she coveted my love.

He took advantage of my trust
And lied to me
And spoke ill of me behind my back
And conspired against me,
Always presenting himself to me
As my friend.
And when I learned the truth
And chose to avoid him,
He felt wronged
And consoled himself
By pronouncing me
A consummate asshole
And a no good sonofabitch.

....

I feel this night
Just like a wind-up mantel clock
When all the might
Has gone from the spring
And gravity has brought
The swinging pendulum to rest.
Oh how I need
The winding key of sleep
To turn tonight
And tighten up the coil in my chest.

I stopped beneath
A great catalpa tree
This morning
On an early walk alone,
The branches bunched
With tiny orchid blooms,
Like clumps of snow,
The ground around my feet
Made almost white by them.
Standing there,
So steeped in shade and scent,
So altogether still,
Enveloped in such loveliness,
I had my heart scooped out
And all the rest
Of my sad being
Clobbered into momentary joy.

....

I picked up a stone.
"You are a great Falcon
Made to take communion with the Sky,"
I said,
And hurled it into the air.
It fell to the earth with a thud.
"What happened?" I asked.
"Why did you not rise and soar?"
"I hate you," said the stone.

Each day the wrinkled lady
Tottered into view,
The huge dog
Burst into a sudden frenzied mix
Of sound and motion,
Roaring up and down the chain link fence
Like something loosed from hell.
The ancient woman
Might have been a bear or fox
For all the furor that she caused.
But after stopping in her tracks
To fix a scolding look
On that great barking thing,
She turned and plodded on.
It didn't seem to bother her.
Oh, she might have been a bit put out
To have her fragile presence
Marked each day
With such ferocious disapproval,
But I believe it pleased her some
To be the cause of such a ruckus,
To know that there was somewhere
In the Cosmos left
Where she could go
And get such certain confirmation
That she was still alive.

Walking through the woods one day
A young boy
Spied a large feather on the ground.
"Oh, wow!" exclaimed the boy!
"What luck!
A feather from a great hawk!"
And he took the feather in his hand
And was struck with wonder,
And inside his wings beat
And he soared
And veered
And dived,
Such was the power
Of the noble feather.
Throughout his life
The feather kept its magic
And never failed
To carry him aloft when he was low
Where he could glide with ease
Upon the high currents,
And never failed
To make him fierce of heart
When he was afraid,
So he could fix his eye
On what he feared.
He lived to be an old man,
This little boy,
And when he died
He soared into the unknown
With the beautiful feather
Clutched in his hand,

Never learning that the magic plume
Had fallen from the broken wing
Of an old turkey
Which had dragged itself into the thick
And died in a tangle of underbrush.

....

You are what you are conscious of.

....

Once upon a time
There lived,
High in the jagged mountains,
In a dark cave,
Alone,
A horrible ogre
Who roared at those
Who dared to take the mountain road
And rolled great boulders
Down on them;
Who had,
Buried somewhere deep inside,
A small lead box
Where he kept locked away
The old memory
Of that great hurt
That demolished his innocence
And butchered out his heart.

The wise man
Does not seek a reason
In the Poet's cryptic line,
But a Rhythm
And a Roundness
And a soft and easy Rhyme.

....

"Don't you want someone to play with?"
Said the teacher
To a small girl
Who was standing by herself
Bouncing a ball
Off the side of the brick building,
Playing a solitary game of pitch and catch.
"Oh, thank you,"
Smiled the girl a little bashfully,
"But I have someone to play with already."

....

The stray cat was scrawny
And seemed to move half sideways
When she walked
And had no tail
And such an ugly face
With eyes so wild and insolent—
I couldn't help but love her.

Imagine this:
You are standing alone
On a hill
In the night.
Suddenly—Poof!
The Earth
And the Moon
And the Sun
Vanish!
Look around
What do you see?
Do you mark the firmament
Beneath your feet
And everywhere you look?
Who are you here,
Enclosed in this great ball
Of interstellar space,
Surrounded by a distant wilderness
Of silent, blinking Stars?
Here,
In this enormous solitude,
Unspeakably remote
From all that you can see,
Are you a bit of isolated consciousness,
Forever locked
Within some cold galactic vault,
Or one Beatified
And safely centered
In a Holy Shrine?

What are we like
In our efforts to comprehend
The meaning of it all?
Like the man
Standing motionless before the Tapestry
That covers the entire wall
Of the great Rotunda,
His feet rooted to the floor,
His nose against the fibers of the cloth,
His eyes confounded
By this point blank view,
Afflicted with the delusion
That somewhere in the blur,
Hidden in the complex weave
Of colored threads,
Is the image
Of his immortal soul.

....

A woman sits on the ground.
She has placed her ego
On a flat rock
And is striking it repeatedly
With a hammer,
Breaking it into a thousand pieces,
Hoping by this violent act of demolition
To make herself presentable to God,
Unconscious of the great conceit
Within herself
That makes the hammer rise and fall.

His denial of the accusation
Was so vigorous
And charged with such moral indignation
And the story he made up
So improbable—
Too improbable not to be true—
That people were persuaded
To believe the lies he told them,
And some were even moved,
Later,
To say how sorry they were
Ever to have doubted him,
And the truth was denounced
As a vicious lie,
And those who told the truth
Were cursed
And hounded from their midst.

....

Not because of the distance
That separates me from other men
Am I lonely,
But because of the distance
That separates me from the Stars.

....

Death came into my house today.
He must have really had it in for me;
He took my cat away.

He did what he did
Because he thought
It was the right thing to do,
Not because he was afraid,
But when the others
Questioned his courage
And treated him with contempt
He began to doubt himself.
"Maybe I did what I did,
Not because it was right,
But because it was safe,
Because I cringed inside somewhere
And lost my nerve."
And he began to believe
What was not true,
And thus it was
That this brave man
Became an abject coward.

....

Every day of my life
I take out my heart,
Hold it in both hands
Above my head,
High as outstretched arms can reach,
And offer it to "God."
It seems that every day
It gains a little weight
And takes more strength
To hoist it up and hold it there,
As if it's turning into lead—

Or gold.
I wonder:
Will I live to see the day
That I can't lift it over my head,
Or will I die with arms
As big and strong
As railroad ties?

....

He sat there,
Motionless and vacant,
Like a corpse
Propped in a chair,
With a pulse and respiration rate.
"What happened to the poor fellow?"
Asked one
Who saw him sitting there like that,
And another answered:
"The finest wiring in his head
Melted together.
You see,
He could not bear to see injustice done
And was compulsively alert."

....

A person who believes in the Messiah
Is, psychologically speaking,
Hard to distinguish from the person
Who believes he is the Messiah.

"What are you looking for?"
Said one
Attending the beautiful young Princess
As she searched the ground
Near the thick stone wall
That surrounded her Kingdom,
Which was an earthly paradise.
"Oh, for a gold locket
That must have slipped from my neck
On our walk last night,"
Answered the young Princess
In a light and almost careless way,
Too ashamed to tell her companion the truth:
That she was looking for a sharp rock
To wedge against her breast
At night,
As she lay still,
Beneath her satin sheets.

....

On the surface
It seemed as if the man
Had committed an honest and harmless act,
Having no deep significance
Or covert purpose.
But there were men of insight and imagination
Who knew about these crafty schemes,
These devious, complicated plots,
And they were able
To see through the subterfuge,
And they told the King of their suspicions

And articulated the details
Of this diabolically clever conspiracy,
And the man was snatched up
And put in the tower
Where he rotted away
With his innocence.

....

A boy stands alone,
Tossing a ball into the air
And catching it
When it comes down—
As it always does.

....

Master, what is life?
It is a soft warm cat
Purring in the lap of a child,
Then mewing at the back door.
Then tearing out the throat
Of a small, tawny rabbit.

....

Most of us go around
Having suffered the opposite fate
Of those who have been buried alive;
We have become the living dead.
And let this be known:
We are not suicides;
We were murdered in warm blood.

I set my foot against the spade
And drove it deep
Into the mound of earth I'd made
And left it standing there
Upright
To rest until
I needed it again,
Which would be soon.
The cold November moon
Was round and bright
And cast the narrow shadow of the spade
Across the ground in front of me,
And in that light
I paused to catch my breath
And watched the steam come off the heap
Of excavated dirt.
She was still soft and warm
That chilly night
When I knelt down
And laid her gently
In the bottom of the hole.
I did not know
That such a little pit
Could be so dark and deep.
The spade stood straight and stiff
And did not start
When I cried out
As if a heavy boot
Had shoved the steel thing
Into my heart.

They were characterized
As ruthless, bloodthirsty, homicidal maniacs
And were charged with crimes against humanity.
The judge put their fate
In the hands of the people,
Who shouted in unison,
As if they were possessed
 Of one great human voice:
"Kill them! Kill them! Kill them!"

....

In a way
We have all been apprehended by Life
And taken into custody,
And dwell,
Each one of us,
On Death row,
Not for a crime we committed,
But because
All that Life seizes
And holds fast
She must at last
Let go.

....

A part of me keeps company
With clowns and rogues;
A part companions with the Stars.

I knelt and put my hand upon the rug
Where just two days ago
My cat lay motionless
And out of life.
I knew the spot would not be warm,
Nor ever warm again,
But there I knelt
And gently placed my hand,
As it to bless the spot,
And paid again the price of love
In full.

....

The wind shoves a lone dry leaf
Down the pavement.
The leaf,
Refusing to be tumbled over
And blown up into the wind,
Braces itself
And skids along
Against the coarse surface,
Making a scraping sound.
Observing this,
The wind throws back
Her lofty head and laughs,
Then reaches down
And with a gusty fingertip
Upends the silly thing
And sets its troubled spirit free.

What is a butterfly
But a worm with wings?
Ahh! But what a difference that!

....

I am a toad,
And often feel
I've swallowed something
Made of lead
Or had a boulder roll on me.
But there are times
I thrill so much inside
I'd swear new Stars
Are forming from my Joy,
And I don't dare
To straighten out my legs
For fear I'll kick the earth
Into another realm!

....

A place enchanted once
And empty of all woe.
My heart is now a cemetery
Which is almost full.

....

Oh to be a hair
From the tail of a horse,
Fixed to the bow
Of Midori's violin.

We have been humanized
Into robotic things,
Civilized into monstrosities.
Oh, to have four hands again,
To get my grasping tail back.
Oh, to swing again
From branch to branch,
To fall asleep again
Safe in the arms
Of a tall tree.

....

The Prince of a shining city
Stands on the brink of a great abyss,
Marshaling all his inner strength
In a last desperate effort
To resist the impulse
To plunge headlong into the void.

....

A man in harmony with his time,
Who keeps a mirror in his house,
Is either blind,
Delusional,
Or consummately able
To confront and deal with
His ignobility and shame.

A mouse,
Placed in a maze
From which there is no escape,
Snoops out every blind
And ends up always
Where he started from,
Then undismayed
Gets turned about
And chases off again,
Trampling futility
Beneath his tiny feet.

....

Once you've been loved by an animal
It's hard to go back to human beings.

....

"Do I love God?" you ask.
"How can you love
What you don't know?"
"Perhaps you can only love
What you don't know,"
He quietly proposed.

....

What is it to me,
Who never suffered condemnation,
That you are moved
To number me among the unredeemed.

Do I feel sorry for the hawk
That lost his prey,
Or happy for the hare
That got away?

....

Almost every adult I know
Is a child who has spoiled,
A little boy or girl gone bad,
And sad to tell
That most of them don't know,
And sadder still
Some do.

....

What scares me most
And makes me most ashamed,
Is watching a crowd of people
And not being able to protect myself
From the realization that I am one of them.

....

We live in a world
Where only those
Who are afflicted with
A comprehensive delusional system
Are well adjusted,
Where only the crazy ones are sane.

I bleed inside
When I see wounded things
And burn
To see injustice done,
Which proves
I still have something to learn.

....

I ceased to be
Long before the buried me,
And if you see me
Walking down the street,
It only proves that ghosts
Are sometimes visible.

....

A man who has feet of clay
Would probably be well advised
To go to a potter
If he required a heart operation.

....

Most of us,
Free and sociable,
Live in solitary confinement.

I've journeyed far from earth
And posed among the beams
Of many distant Stars.
Yet still I'm plagued
With ancient memories
And prehistoric dreams.

....

You know you're sensitivity has run amuck
When you stand bundled up
Outside your house,
A hungry stove inside,
Leaning on the handle of your splitting maul,
So taken by the toughness
Of the stock of wood in front of you,
The beauty of the grain,
That you can't bring yourself
To batter it apart
And turn it into fuel.
"I'm not that cold," you say,
And set the piece aside.
"I wonder if I'll be so warm of heart,
Some other day
When Mr. Cold is trying on my house for size
And there's not other wood."

....

Only when you find out who you are not
Will you discover who you are.

Ah! It happened today!
We received a message
From intelligent beings
Living on a planet
Out there somewhere
In the blurred immensity
Of our own Milky Way,
Sent out to us
While we were still in prehistoric times.
I wonder,
Will they still be there
Ten thousand years from now
When our reply arrives—
And will we still be here?

....

A small enchanted bird
With feats of acrobatic wonder
Works a magic weave of flight
Among the scattered soldiery of trees,
Until she sees
Reflected in the heavy full-length plate
Of cabin glass
A shadow forest realm yet unexplored,
And on an impulse
Bred into her airy blood
Tilts her wings
And plunges wild-eyed
Into that glassy world
Of mirrored possibilities.

They frighten me,
The people that I meet,
Even when they smile,
Especially when they smile.

....

When one man comes upon
A distinguished colleague of his
Sweeping the streets,
He is dismayed.
"Good sir,
This is beneath your dignity," he says.
The sweeper looks up at him
And smiles wisely.
"No, my old friend.
Don't you see:
This gives me dignity."

....

She did everything she could
To make him think
That something was amiss,
That she had not been true,
And when he finally approached her
With his suspicions
She was dismayed and positively indignant
That he could even imagine such a thing.

I have retired
And am no longer
A contributing member of society,
Which gives me a good feeling.

....

As he was being led away
From the brutal massacre,
A survivor looked back
At those who had been slaughtered
And at those who lay mutilated
In the smoking wreckage,
And sighed with impious gratitude:
"Oh thank you, merciful God."

....

Not the trap,
Not the people who make the trap,
Not even the people who set the trap;
It's the people who buy the soft warm hats
Who slaughter the White Fox
In the raw Alaskan snow.

....

I ease my weary bark into the water,
Which is dark and deep,
And step inside
And glide into the silent currents
That carry me to sleep.

The calamity of becoming an adult
Is not in finding,
After a heavy January snow,
That you are restrained
By rules of appropriate behavior
From going out and playing in it,
But in discovering
That you no longer want to.

....

I cannot tell you where my youth has fled.
I only know the days that were
Are covered over with the dust
Of many vague and doubtful years,
And heavy rust
Has ruined the runners of my sled.

....

I live now in a haunted house,
And the ghost that moves about
And makes things bump and glow
In late and early hours
And in the hours in between—
Is me.

....

The night sky
Is a choir of small white voices
That sing to those
Who have eyes that hear.

To the questing man
An angel appeared and said,
"Come and I will take you to God
And if you are willing
To put your Wonder up in trade
He will shed his Light
On all that in your heart is dark
And render clear to you
All that in your mind is vague."
"Return to God," said the questing man.
"Tell him he drives too hard a bargain."

....

She was so kind,
So thoughtful,
So impeccably virtuous
That many of her good neighbors
Found it unsettling to discover
That deep inside they hated her.

....

When I was still a young boy
I discovered the word *dog*
Spelled backwards
Made the word God,
And though I have lived
A good many years since then,
I have not found
A more admirable theology than that.

The flowers sleep
Beneath a heavy quilt of January snow
And dream of that enchanted spring
Which was
And will not come again.

....

I looked into a mirror.
I saw a fool.
"What does a mirror know?"
I said.

....

An old man sat on a park bench,
Sobbing.
A little boy approached,
Stopped right next to the man,
Reached out
And put a small hand on his knee
And asked,
"Why are you crying?
Did you hurt yourself?"
The old man smiled through his tears.
"I have memories that hurt," he said.
"Are they very bad memories?"
Asked the little boy.
"Oh, no. They are all very good,"
Sighed the old man.

The do-gooders
Do one good deed after another.
It's what they are supposed to do,
And does them good.

....

Two men:
One gusted through life
As if his coat were cut from a sail;
The other sat in a cemetery,
Dressed in a shroud.
I knew them both.

....

"But the bars are only made of balsa wood,"
Said a small vivid bird
Sitting on a twig of a nearby tree
To a gloomy lion
Prowling about in his cage.
"Only balsa wood painted black
To look like iron bars.
Why you could jump right through them
If you wanted to."
At this the lion stopped,
Fixed a steely eye on his tormentor,
Then threw back his great mane
And roared ferociously,
Which frightened the vivid bird away.

Angelic apparitions
Clad in misty white
Appear to those
Whose heart is caught
And crushed in night.

....

It is difficult for a fish
Confined in a bowl of shallow water
Nestled in the middle of a vast desert
To dream of waters
Dark and deep.

....

Two things plague the ancient heart:
Remembered wounds,
Both given and received,
And memories that are good.

....

I did not see the doe,
Heard only in the wooded thick
Her low harrumph.
I could not go to her
In her deep shadowed realm,
And so I sat alone and sighed
To know that she was there,
So near to me
And I was here
So utterly remote to her.

Out of the tumult,
Rent with wails
And desperate shrieking prayers,
A panic stricken man fought his way
And clambered over a fence
To escape the frenzy
Where he came face to face
With an aged woman calmly tending her roses.
The man looked at her in dismay.
"My God, woman! Haven't you heard?
The world is coming to an end!"
"Oh, yes, yes. I've heard,"
Answered the woman
In a voice fresh and calm and soft
As the petal of a rose.
"Will you please hand me the watering can
There by the bench."

....

My heart's become a cave
That's dark and cold
And holds the bones of something
Once bright and bold.

....

Any man can be immortal
While he is alive.

Late in the day
Two toads sat in the dust facing each other,
Both downcast,
Croaking about the dreary pointlessness of life,
When of a sudden
One of the toads
Ceased his somber croaking
And his eyes became fixed
And glistened with incredulity,
And his face fell under a spell
And began to glow.
Then in a hushed voice he said,
"Oh, my god! It cannot be!
And yet my eyes confirm it's so!
Not far behind you is a loveliness
Such as I have never seen before.
Surely it is Fairy
From a land of make believe,
Or some other airy creature
From a bright and distant realm."
The lips of the toad
Barely moved as he spoke
So fearful he was
Of startling the vision away,
And then in a whisper
He urged his friend to turn his head,
Ever so slowly,
That he too could see
The enchanted presence.
But when the other toad
Finally got his head eased round

All he saw was a warty lizard
Sitting on a rock
Reflecting a golden sheen
Caused by the slanting rays
Of the evening sun.
When he turned back
His companion was still in a swoon
And his brown skin
Had turned into a blue tunic
And his glow had brightened
To a radiance.
"It is truly some angelic thing
Not of this dusty world,"
Lied the road who was still brown,
And he felt profoundly sorry for his friend.
But that night
When he closed his dreary eyes and slept.
He dreamed himself
Of something from another world
That so bedazzled him
That he determined
He would rather die than wake.

....

The human heart has a long shelf life,
But even a great heart can spoil
If left too long in the cupboard,
And become unfit to put on the table.

"Saul," said God,
"Before the foundation of the world
I chose you
To be a child in my Kingdom.
Long before you were ever born
I gave you the gift of my Grace,
Because it pleased me to."
"But what of my dear friend, Malachi.
Did you also choose him?"
"No. Saul. I did not choose Malachi."
"But why, God?
He is as good and as wise
And as kind and just as I,
And my love for him is so great
That knowing he is lost
Turns all the joy
That should now fill my heart
To bitter grief."
And Saul began to weep.
"Oh, God,
Why before the foundation of the world,
Long before he was ever born,
Did it not please you
To give the gift of your Grace To Malachi?"

....

I could not love thee, "God," so much
Had she not scorned to love me more;
The heart I carry in my hands to thee
I carried first to her who slighted me.

Everything beautiful
Is ultimately sad.

....

The longing heart
Can swell to such degree
The chest itself
Must stretch to greater round,
And finally in
The vast expanse of space
Is yet not space enough
To keep it bound.

And such a hunger
Can the sick heart know
That loaf of stone
Will it attempt to carve,
And if at last
No nourishment is found,
Then it will feed upon itself—
Or starve.

And when at last
The last of hope is gone
The dying heart
Will shudder and go still
And none will ever know
Or ever guess
The empty cup
That longed so much to fill.

There's a bell
Attached to the door of my heart
Which rings
Only on those rare occasions
When I go out
And when I return—
Alone.

....

He had melted down his virtue
And his strength
And his courage
And made of it a great sword
To hold against his need
Which had become a beast
That would devour him,
But when his passion came
The great sword wilted in his hand
And he was seized
By the mouth of the beast
And consumed.

....

The first sifting of autumn snow
Whitens unraked leaves
This cold November morn,
And standing
Looking down at that fine cast
Of crystal white
Scattered on the brown remains of fall

Something swells in me
That's long ago and glad,
And something sinks in me
That's now
And oh so very sad.

....

The early morning air
Was bone cold
And a heavy frost
Brittled the winter grass
And crusted on the bare trees,
And the world seemed steeped
In a gray, frigid stillness,
And there,
Fouled in the dark bramblework
Of a far tree,
Round and white and luminous,
Looking like a great pearl
Caught in a branchy net,
The morning Moon!
A Bright sight
To these old wintry eyes,
A welcome glow
To this December heart.

....

It does no good to push against a door
That opens only in.

The rank Morning Glory
Sacked my rose plant almost overnight
And slew the late September rose,
But oh the bloom
That birthed upon that wild vine!
Should cultured flowers everywhere
Die and never come to life again
That this too fair a blossom
Have its day,
It were a happy, happy trade.

....

Ten thousand distant suns
Shine down on me
This quiet moonless night
With passionate indifference,
Devoid of grace;
Ten thousand streams
Of incandescent light
Converge upon
Yet have not power to warm
My upturned face.

....

Because of its complete indifference
To good and evil
And love and hate
And life and death
And to all things beautiful and otherwise,
I admire the rock.

Every day Beauty approaches me
And smiles softly
Like an angel
And takes me by the hand
And leans close
And lays her lips upon my cheek,
And then she puts her mouth to my ear
And whispers into it a single word,
Always the same single word:
"Joy," she whispers.
But then she puts her mouth
To my other ear
And again whispers a single word,
Always the same word:
"Sorrow," she whispers,
And when she leaves
I always find something dead
In my pocket.

....

On hearing that the human race
Had become extinct
One near to God asked Him:
"How could you allow Mankind
To perish from the planet Earth?"
"Allow' is not quite the right word,"
Replied the Almighty;
"I caused it to happen.
You see it was either man
Or the Spotted Owl."

One year ago today
She sailed down the side of a mountain
Like something made out of magic,
Making the snow hiss
And leaving in her wake
The sudden tracks
Of skis waxed with wonder.
And now from the doorway
We see her sitting there
 Rigged to a complicated chair
Holding a brush in her teeth,
Straining to smudge into round
On the canvas propped in front of her
A Yellow Sun.
"Isn't it unbelievably sad?"
Sighed my friend
"Oh, no,"
I answered softly,
Feeling something yellow on my face;
"I think it's glorious!"

. . . .

As she browsed carefree
Among the flowers
That grew along the meadow's edge,
Her heart aglow,
She could not know
That in the woods that loomed nearby,
Sitting wedged in a high tree,
The Archer had fixed his eye
On her fair breast

And drawn back his bow.
She could not know,
That as she stopped
And tilted back her head
And shook her hair
That at that very moment
The Archer's fingers
Loosened on the string
And let the arrow go.

....

On thinking of the choice Eve made,
To take the apple from the serpent
And eat of it, I wonder:
Did Eve really have a choice?
Could she,
By an act of free will,
Really choose to do something
That would contradict
God's perfect foreknowledge
Of what she would do?
Whose was it,
The original sin ?

....

What good to close and bar the door
And brick the windows up
When what you fear
And hope to keep outside
Lies lurking underneath your bed.

Sitting there
Listening to the fantastic tales
The old man told
Of the great battles he had fought
And the long, long odds he had overcome,
And of his many narrow escapes
And his mighty deeds of derring-do,
The listener struggled
To keep a straight face,
Feigning wide-eyed wonder
At everything he heard.
Inwardly he thought,
"The poor old devil
Lives in a world of delusion,
A world of dreams
That did not come true.
Here,
Talking to me now,
He becomes the gallant paladin
He might have been."
And he pitied the poor fellow,
And it did not occur to him
That everything the storyteller said—
Was true!

....

When one of two men,
Leaning against each other to stand erect,
Falls,
How shall the other remain upright?

The great presumption,
The great blasphemy:
That God made man in his own image.

....

From time to time
I see this woman in the marketplace
Who always moves about alone
And always wears a smile on her face,
Which sometimes looks
More like an impish grin,
As if she's just pulled off
Some kind of prank
And is getting away with it,
Or like the smile
Of one bemused inside
By some delightful thought
That clowns around upon the porch
Of her unconscious mind.
Perhaps the droll expression on her face
Means simply that she's tapped into
A spring of happy water
That bubbles up inside
And makes her always glad,
Or just as like,
The smile she shows
Is nothing but a deep disguise
To hide the fact
That she is always sad.

Ah! That I am here,
In this one place,
Yet everywhere at once;
And now,
In this one present moment fixed,
Yet lost in time;
And all alone,
Yet one with all!

....

A mourning dove
Lies dead on the sidewalk.
Her mate mills about,
Bobbing his head,
Waiting,
Making small noises,
Now and then inspecting the gray body,
Nudging it with its beak.
All day the vigil lasts,
And darkness falls.
I see them both near the midnight hour
Dimly in the lamplight,
And when I wake,
In the dim light of dawn
I see them both.
When hope finally dies
And lies down by the fallen dove,
The mate binds up his love and leaves,
And I go over to collect the body.

My heart beats quick and bright.
My blood is all aglow.
I wake from dark,
And light is all I know.
I feel inside
As if I've fused with all that's good,
Or fallen in love with God!!

....

Pity the man who survives the death
Of his most vital delusion.

....

It is quite possible
That the light of a dim star
That passes through your telescope
And into the black center of your eye
Is from a star that died
Ten thousand years ago;
Of course,
It is quite possible
That could your telescope
Find out a place devoid of light,
That there ten thousand years ago
A star was born
And is just now
About to find its way
Into your eye.

"Rabbi," asked the child:
"Is there a God?"
"Child," answered the Rabbi:
"There is only God."

....

All that is, I Am,
Yet one with nothingness am I.
On the bench of my being
Now and Nevermore
Sit side by side,
And on the Bright pavilion
Of my Consciousness
Life and Death
Join hands and Dance.

....

I came upon a Wayfarer
Stumbling from the brambles,
His flesh torn and bleeding.
"Excuse me, Sir,
But why do you move among the sharp thorns
When there is a trodden path so near?
Have you lost your way?"
"Yes, in my muse I must have wondered off,"
Whereupon he turned
And disappeared again into the dense undergrowth.

I followed after him,
Fighting the briars that tore at me.

"Wait!" I cried. "Are you mad?
Please turn around before it is too late
And you are lost again."
From some yards in front
He heard the Wayfarer call back,
"I have already acted upon that wisdom. Sir."

Undeterred, I followed after him.
"You are surely mad!" I yelled.
"I cannot let you harm yourself.
I beg you to return with me
To the safety of the open road,"
To which he answered,
"Sir, there is no danger here
That can compare to the snares and tangles
Of the trodden way."
With that, I despaired for the poor soul
And returned to join my companions
On the beaten path.

....

A spider browsed in its web,
And wondered at the sticky snare she had made.
"What if it were I
Caught in this web of my own spinning," she mused.
And it made her smile to wonder this.
But when she next sought to move about
She found that she was stuck fast,
And a terrible fear possessed her,
And she struggled mightily,
But to no avail.

Forever, until this very moment,
A spirit groped blind and mindless in the Dark.
Then he felt something placed in his hand
And felt his eyes tingle
And his mind open.
And it was a Bright Lamp
He found in his hand.
"What Miracle is this?" he exclaimed, amazed.
"And what wonders are these?"
And he rejoiced at the Marvels
He could see
And the wonders he could comprehend.
But ere long he felt a tug at the lamp,
And his hand loosened involuntarily,
And his eyes and mind closed,
And he became again,
Forever,
A spirit groping blind and mindless in the Dark.

....

A child wandered the ground
And came upon a deep Hole,
And wondered it,
Then took a rock in her hand
And dropped it into the Darkness
And angled her ear
And listened with all her might
But heard only an emptiness.
She tried again.
Nothing.
Then from deep in the Hole

She heard a voice utter her name,
And was seized by a great fear
And ran away.

The years sped,
 And now rudely marked by time,
She came back to the Hole again
And again she heard her name uttered,
But this time it was a beckon that she heard.
And she found that she was no longer struck with fear—
And stepped into it.

....

A woman sits on a bench in the park,
Her face in a book.
Being preoccupied with my mortality,
As I often am,
It occurs to me that surely such a woman would know.
And I approach and sit next to her.
"Excuse me, wise lady,
Can you tell me if there is life after death?"
She turns her head and peers into my eyes,
Focused, it seems to me,
On something just beyond the back of my head.
Then turns back to her book.
And after a moment, replies:
"Do you mean to say, 'Is there Life after This?'"
I thank her and graciously take my leave,
Feeling as if a frantic bat
has been loosed in my head.

A warty toad squats on a sodden log,
Quiet and motionless,
And on a supple branch above him
A Brightly Colored song bird bobs.
"Why are you so morose?" the song bird chirps.
"It is likely," replied the toad,
"I would be more cheerful
If I were brightly colored
And sitting on a supple branch—
About to sing
Or vault into the air."
The heart of the song bird then felt a painful stab,
And she was ashamed.
"I'm sorry, Toad," she said.
"Please do not pity me," he croaked.
Then the songbird fluttered down to the sodden log
And stood beside the warty Toad
And began, with her songs,
To teach him how to love—
And how to dream.

(Now you may think in time the Frog became a Brightly Colored bird, and the two flew off together into the green wood; but it is just as like the Brightly Colored bird became a warty toad, and to this day they sit together on the sodden log—though both are exceedingly unlikely.)

A horrifying beast
Sleeps in a cave
And when hunger and thirst
Wake it from its ferocious dreams
It lurches forth
And feasts on human flesh
And guzzles human blood.
It is not so much the hunger
That frenzies the beast
But a menace inside
Born of ignorance and fear—
Called Hatred.
And the beast is called War.

....

I heard a man today
Being lauded for something he had done.
"Isn't all this rather humbling?"
He was asked.
He blushed and laughed
And full of conceit
Agreed that it was.

....

A novice asks the master
How he will know
When he has achieved the Way?
And the Master answers,
"When you can see through a mirror."

In the green meadow
A flock of wooly sheep
Graze on the grassy flowers
Unaware that in the nearby woods
A hungry wolf
Has drawn back his ears.
The sheep do not choose to be gentle
Nor the wolf to thirst for blood—
Nor the farmer,
Waiting in stillness with his gun,
To squeeze the trigger.
The shot that rings out,
Startles the sheep
And shatters more than the silence.

....

I watched a small child at play.
Perhaps you can guess why
It made me weep.

....

He loves me too much to let go,
But I fear he is too old and weak
To last the night.
He's all used up.
I have invited Death into my house,
To do what he does.
I treat him kindly,
Make him feel welcome.
I have asked a great favor of him.

When I wake in the morning
I pray to find his work done,
My cat at peace.
But in the morning
I find Death gone
And Handsome Cat
Still curled on the quilt.
Now I must act
To do myself what Death declined to do.
I love him too much
Not to let go.

Handsome Cat is finished.
I saw to it this morning,
Carried him to the doctor's
Wrapped in a clean blue towel.
The doctor's drugs were soft and quick.
In a way we cheated Death,
Who often likes to torment and prolong.
Oh, he died all right,
But so gently, so very very gently.
He simply "fell asleep" in my arms,
As a drowsy lamb might fall asleep
Nestled in its mother's wool—

The clean blue towel was light
With what there was of Handsome Cat
When I arrived,
But oh the weight of it when I returned.

I stood alone in the night
And harkened to the tolling of a distant bell.
The night was cold, the air thick with falling snow.
So softly it tolled
I almost doubted that it tolled at all.
I bent my ear and listened with such keen intent
That I began to fancy that it tolled for me.
I smiled at myself to have a thought like that.
And yet the soft hushed sound of it
Seemed almost to seek the hollow of my ear
As for a place to rest—or sleep.
And then a sudden rush of wind
Took the sound away.

....

Emerging from a vast expanse of sand,
A woman staggers to a wayside well,
Parched and desperate,
Her mouth a dry burrow,
But hope now beginning to gurgle up in her.
"It is a Godsend," she gasps,
As she bends and peers into it
And sees her face
Reflected some 15 meters down.
It will be some moments
Before she discovers
That something very vital
Is missing from the well.

I browse among the weathered stones
And ponder the names and dates
Of those who used to be
But are no more.
They remind me of closed books
That will never be opened again,
Stories that are only told once.
And each one read by just a few,
And then those few…

....

People said
The old man was just plain mean,
That he kept a dragon in his heart
And that the dragon no doubt felt right at home
In that dark cavern place.
It never occurred to them
That there really was a dragon—
A fierce dragon—
And that it kept the man
From reaching a treasure of love
Buried deep in his heart.

....

Try to be to others
What I have tried to be to you:
Both a window and a mirror.

By sheer chance—
But almost as if by agreement—
Two men meet in a small clearing,
Each desperately lost.
"Come with me," said one.
"We will have a better chance together."
The other agrees.
But as they confront the wilderness again
They can't agree which way to go.
They argue for some time
Until they agree again—
This time to go their separate ways.

....

The mouse can smell the cheese,
And with admirable energy
Works the complicated maze.
Hour after hour he works,
Turned back by every blind.
He's a very discerning mouse
And finally sees that he has left his prints
On every channeled "way,"
But he persists,
Until finally he gets it into his small gray head
That he is being gamed
And quits playing.
But not long after that
He's up and running again,
Powered more by the need to run—
Than by the need to eat.

When I am gone
Remember only this of me:
That I reverenced Beauty!
Was desperate for Truth!
Tried to do Good!
And Loved as few have ever loved
(Yes, and grieved as few have ever grieved).
But on balance
My life was a draft of dark red wine
Which I drank gladly,
Then crushed the glass beneath my foot.

....

A surly old woman
Stands at the window of a garden shop,
Gazing pensively at a spiny cactus
Squatting in a pot of clay.
A shift of focus in her eyes
Confronts her with her own reflected image in the glass.
"Harrumph!!" she mutters
And turns away.

....

A star falls from the sky.
A child picks it up
And puts it in his pocket.
At length he becomes an old man,
And when he dies
They find something
Sparkling in the palm of his hand.

A man lies dying.
A rabbi is present.
"Are you comfortable?" he asks.
"Is there anything I can do for you?"
"I am quite at ease, thank you."
The rabbi asks if the dying has made his peace with God,
And the man answers,
"I don't believe in God, not as you do, Rabbi."
And when asked if he has any fear,
The dying man looks up into the Rabbi's eyes
And only smiles softly in reply.
"Would you mind if I pray?" the Rabbi asks.
The man sighs peacefully.
"I'd rather you didn't," he says
And explains
That his whole life has been a prayer of sorts—
"A Communion," he says.
His eyes fall closed.
The Rabbi is silent
And looks at his hands in his lap.
"I'm afraid you have me at a painful disadvantage, Sir.
Will you be kind enough to excuse me?"

....

"I don't believe in magic," said the child.
"I know it's just all tricks."
I asked the child if he thought
That a hummingbird were a trick
Or the Sun or the moon
Or the Stars in the night sky.
The child puzzled this for a long time.

Then his eyes widened
And his arms spread out,
"Maybe it's All Magic!
Is that what you mean?"
Then it was my turn to puzzle.
And after a few moments
I put my hand on the child's head and said,
"Let's just say:
It's all Mystery!"

[I didn't say this to the child,
But thought it:
"We all know
That you can't pull a rabbit out of a hat,
But when you get right down
To the very bottom of trying to explain
Where a rabbit comes from,
Well, maybe that explanation
Is not so far fetched after all."]

....

I dreamed I died
And when "I woke"
I found it wasn't a dream after all.
But how to describe this strange "waking"?
Like a warbled song
Finding its way
Back into the throat of a bird,
Or a snowflake rising
Back into the cloud
From which it fell.

A sordid bunch of clothing
Huddles in an alcove between two buildings
Knees drawn up,
Arms clutching the knees,
Drawn up like that, I guess,
To guard against the cold—
Or maybe just to have something
To put her arms around.

....

The right answer to the ultimate question is YES—
That is, IF you get the ultimate question right.

....

Outside.
Deep into Night.
An effusion of Stars.
A bright Moon.
It's the Moon that wonders me,
The reflected light of it.
Without the witness of the Moon
We would not know
The "Darkness" it moves through
Is filled with Light!!

(I am also wondered by my eyes
That really see so little of the Light.
That know, but cannot "see,"
The Brightness in the Night)

Sometimes I feel like the thing
That gives an anvil a sense of purpose.
Sometimes like a pair of wings
Attached to a brightly Colored Bird.

....

I wonder which is worse:
Seeing things that aren't there
And believing that they are.
Or not seeing things that are.
And believing that they aren't.

....

I see a man moving in a circle.
"What are you up to, good man?" I ask.
The walker explains
That he used to move
In a perfectly straight line.
"But now I have changed all that," he twinkles.
I leave him there making his "rounds"
Content to pursue
My own erratic way.

....

The day is on the verge of breaking.
She has shivered through the night.
She tries with all her failing might
But cannot stop the shaking.
"Oh, hurry, Sun!"

A man stands before a judgmental God.
"You have failed me, my child," She says.
The man is exceedingly perplexed.
"But that's not possible," he protests
"I repented all my sins,
Ended every day with a prayer,
And always put you first in my life."
God regarded him sadly and said,
"When you were born
I invested you with Love."
"Yes, I know" the man said,
And he began to brighten.
"And I have always kept it safe in my heart."
God looked at him and sighed:
"That is where you have failed me."

....

When scientists discover life "out there"
It will be a monumental event in human history,
But will come as no surprise to me,
For the Cosmos is awash in life!
(I have a way of knowing such things)
Here's a thought:
Maybe there's a planet out there
Where life evolved
That has already discovered
Life "out there"
And the life they discovered "out there"—
They discovered HERE!

Two Grave Diggers
Three feet down.
Pitching out the broken ground.
One grubs,
"Do you know who this one's for?"
The second grubs back,
"Don't have the faintest.
Do you really care?"
"No, don't' care at all—
Just wonderin's all."
"Damn this is tough dirt!" the second grouses.
The first stands up straight
And leans on his long-handled spade
To catch his breath.
He looks around
To see if any visitors are about,
Sees only a community of weathered stones.
Then sighs and goes back to work.

....

I'm moved to sing.
I open my mouth
But cannot make a sound.
My lips are made of clay,
My throat asleep.
"Maybe it's because,
I have no song in my heart," I think,
"But why then would I be moved to sing?"

A human body has trillions and trillions of cells.
And a common cell has 100 trillion atoms.
Atoms.
Impossibly small.
Nucleus 10,000 times smaller than the atom itself!!!!
In this nucleus protons and neutrons.
Too small to imagine.
Inside them "things" called quarks.
Several "flavors".
Most common—"up" and "down" ones.
Electrical charge, color charge, spin, and mass.
When you understand
The mysterious ways of these infinitesimals,
Then you will know that you are on the very verge
Of meeting "God."

....

Strange
That John the Baptist
Who recognized Jesus as the long-awaited One
And baptized him
In the river Jordan,
(Where the holy spirit descended as a dove
And a voice from heaven proclaimed,
"This is my beloved son with whom I am well pleased.")
Would later,
Waiting execution in a prison cell,
Write a note to Jesus
Asking if he were the One
"Or shall we look for another."
It's also strange

How this problematic fragment
Survived the long redaction process
By the many scribes
Who were intent on portraying Jesus
As the long-awaited One.

....

In addition to the two
Great commandments
Is a third:
"Judge not."
Who judges himself,
Or another,
Judges God.

....

I have also often wondered
Why, when Jesus appears
After the crucifixion,
He is not immediately recognized
By those who encounter him—
(On the shore of Lake Tiberias.
On the road to Emmaus...)
Even the beloved Mary Magdalene,
Seeing him outside the tomb,
Thinks he is the gardener.
Why was Jesus moving about
Appearing in disguise?

A discouraged woman
Gropes her way
Through the dark of her Night.
Suddenly she sees a Brightness
Weaving through the dark.
"It is a guiding light," she sighs,
And follows after it...
But she can't keep up
And eventually loses sight of it.
"It is enough to know it's there," she says,
And her courage comes back
And she goes on groping her way.

....

I think the answer to the question:
"What is the greatest biological disaster of all time?"
Will be answered in the near future.

....

A Rabbi and a companion
Walk from a gathering.
"Did you notice, Rabbi,
The ugly smudge
On that man's garment?"
For a moment or two
The Rabbi does not answer,
Then says,
"I saw no blemish on his robe.
Perhaps the smudge you saw
Is in your eye."

A hundred short years from now
I will have been dead for over eighty years.
And virtually all the 8 billion people
Who now have a pulse
Will be keeping me company,
Including, of course,
My children
And their children,
And perhaps the children of their children.
Make haste to be kind!

....

I stand and watch a great procession pass.
There seems no end to it—
The staggering multitude of suffering humanity—
The sick, the abused, the tormented, the maimed, the hungry,
the weak...
Shuffling along, slouched, broken—ruined.
Off to the side
Sitting beneath a blossoming tree
I see a mystic
Looking the other way
Communing with the All of Everything.
And over a hill
I hear hymns of praise and thanksgiving
Coming from a little village church.
And listen! There! Can you hear it?
I believe that's the gladsome song of a lark!

White contends with Black
On Armageddon Plain
To settle the matter once and for all.
They clinch and grapple
And snarl and bite and shriek,
Sending up a great commotion of dust.
Finally it is over,
And when the air clears
Only a heap of Gray remains.

....

Two men pause along their way.
"Maybe it's all a joke," offers one.
"If it's all a joke,
Why am I not laughing?" asks the other.
"Maybe you don't understand the joke."
"And I suppose you do?"
"No I don't understand it either,
That's why I'm not laughing."
They start to move again.
"Maybe it's not all a joke,
Maybe we should take it seriously."
They stop and look at each other
And break out laughing.

....

I wonder what I'd wonder
If I'd wondered all to Light;
I wonder what would get me through
That dark and dreamless night.

Every advance in science
Is a move toward God.

....

As I am walking down a barren way
I see ahead of me
Atop a large rock
Three fearsome birds
All dressed in black,
Tearing at something with their beaks.
"Some hapless rodent," I sigh.
They scatter as I approach,
And when I hazard a look at the torn remains
I am dismayed to find
The gruesome carcass
Is actually what is left of a human heart!!
You can imagine my horror!
Aghast, I turn away and leave.
And not far down the path
I come upon a man
Lying face down in the dirt
Sobbing violently
And beating the earth with his fists.
I go up to him
And ask if there is something I can do.
"Leave me alone!" he shrieks.
"I have just lost the only thing in this world that I love."
It is only then that I notice
The blood on his hands
And the ground red beneath him.

I meet an ancient soldier
From the last great war—
Battle of the Bulge.
He talks of it,
But only just a little.
No sign that he's been wounded,
Except that when I take my leave
He lifts his face
And looks me in the eyes.
Every soldier is a casualty of war.

....

From a nameless derelict,
Standing on a corner
With a sign asking for help,
To an overnight sensation,
Recognized the world over.
A fairy tale come true!
Or a tale of woe to come?

....

He flies the Jolly Roger
And prowls the skies of night
Not drawn to the gloomy Dark
But on the hunt for Light.
A cutlass dangles from his side
An earring from his ear
He steers uncharted "waters"
But has no fear.

We're all just creatures
Struggling to survive,
Like every other creature
Great or small,
But we're the only one that cries,
The only one that knows he dies
Once and for all.

....

When the last of all questions is answered
And the last of all battles is won—
And the final adventure is over
And the last of our labors is done,
What then?

....

If every sparkle in the sky
Should suddenly expire,
Some years would pass
Before an earthly eye
Could tell that one was gone,
And let a thousand years go by
And still a plenitude of stars
Would sparkle in a shepherd's sky.

....

Some things are just too damn precious to die—
And yet they do.

It's very important to teach a child "No!"—
And later how to say, "No."
But it's vital the child learns
The power and the glory
Of saying, "Yes!"

....

Retired. Unmarried. Reclusive.
His invalid mother upstairs
An open wound in her chest.
Unable to leave her bed.
Dying—breast cancer.
He's lived with her for years,
The mother an old dear friend of mine.
Every Sunday morning
A mitzvah bag
Left on the front door for her.
Some special pastry treat,
A pound of ground coffee,
Chocolate, etc.
This little gifting done for years.
A heart attack—the son.
Five days pass
Before the bodies are found.
Inside the front door,
Tossed in a corner,
Each still holding its little gift,
A careless heap
Of mitzvah bags—
Never carried up the stairs.

So grossly many
Scourged and scorned and crucified—
Before Golgotha.
So grossly many since.
Before we're done
Some watcher from a distant star
Might name this one-time garden Earth
The Place of the Skull.

....

Inside every child,
In separate cells,
Two spirits are confined,
One an angel
Reaching through the bars.
One a demon
Tearing at the lock.

....

There are lots of foul words
In the language of man
That are ugly and vile and cruel,
But of all the worst the worst of them all—
Is this charge from the mouth of a Ghoul—
Heresy!

An excited little girl
Sits by the bed of her Grandfather.
She is telling him
That their teacher took them
To see the Statue of Equality today.
(The old one it replaced
Was "falling apart" and "outdated")
Before he "falls asleep"
He raises a feeble hand
And gestures her to come closer
And when she has
He whispers to her
That it used to be called the Statue of Liberty
And that it beckoned to all
Who were "Yearning to be Free."
"Promise me you'll never forget that," he said.
She is a little confused,
But she puts her head on his chest
And feels his arm go over her:
"I won't forget, Papa.
I promise."

....

At first they only dreamed of being Free
And then they schemed
And then they took up arms...
And blood was shed
And many graves were made,
But finally they prevailed,
And a new flag of Freedom was posted on a hill,
And all pledged allegiance to it

And they wrote an Anthem
And all would stand and place a hand on their heart
Whenever it was sung,
And eyes would fill with tears to hear it,
And they vowed to remain strong and always vigilant.
And they prospered and were happy
For a long time...
You may wonder how it was
That they lost the precious Freedom
Their fathers had sacrificed their lives to win.
And you might think
It had to be torn away from them,
That other captors came and took it away—
And some will say that's just what happened—
But the sad truth is this:
Little by little,
Not knowing what they were doing,
They gave it all away—
And slipped into a joyless servitude...

But their Despair was not complete,
For some of the old are starting to remember
And some of the young are starting to dream again.

....

An old wolf caught in a steel trap
Gnawing at his leg
Grips and tears at my heart,
More than a young child
Fighting for his life.

She did not believe in God,
Not as most believe in God,
And therefore thought that prayer
Was just a self-indulgence of the weak.
"They need to pray," she thought.
And when her nights were long and dark,
No one ever suspected...
Which raises this curious question:
If God exists,
And is responsive to believers who pray,
How does God respond
To the "prayers" of those
Who don't believe?

....

If Nostradamus were truly
The great prognosticator that people think,
Why did he,
When he was trying to decide
Which of his three sons
To leave his fortune to,
Decide to leave it to the first one
To survive into adulthood?
Surely he could have predicted that.

....

I belong to myself.
I am my own.
Let me Be!!.

A song bird sits
On high branch of a tree
And is about to warble out
Her hymn to the break of day
When she sees
In the cover of new-fallen snow
Tracks which she does not recognize.
What is most curious to her
Is that the tracks
Just start out of nowhere!
"Now how can that be," she puzzles to herself.
"Tracks just don't begin in an open field of snow like that—
Birds, of course, but those tracks weren't made by a bird."
And she determines to look into the matter.
After she ruffles the white dusting from her back
And the stiffness from her joints,
She jumps into the air
And flies off following the tracks,
But when, to her amazement,
Right in the middle of the field,
They just stop
As mysteriously as they began,
She veers
And wings her way back
To the tree,
And after a brief wondering
She flutters away her perplexity
And breaks into her morning song.

No herebefore,
No hereafter,
Only here.
Only now!!
This Present.
Celebrate it with every breath
With every pulse.
Let every atom in your body sing!!
There is no second coming.

....

It's a long, long journey from the Darkness
Into the Light of Day,
From barbarism and servitude
To civility and freedom—
But a very short return trip.

....

It almost goes without saying
That our thoughts can affect
Our moods, motivations, attitudes, etc.
Positive thoughts make us more positive
And negative thoughts make us more negative.
(Exactly how this happens
Is still something of a mystery, I think)
But can our thoughts
Really alter the molecular structure
Of the water in our brains,
As some are now affirming?
And can that altered water

Then alter our consciousness?
Is that how it works—
The power of positive and negative thinking?
We think beautiful thoughts;
The beautiful thoughts make our water molecules beautiful;
And the beautiful water
Then makes us more beautiful?
Or is it a little more complicated than that?

I'm gently mocking here,
And I shouldn't be.
For it's likely the explanation of thought dynamics
And consciousness alteration
Is going to challenge our current ability to understand,
And I don't want to laugh at something
That might be true
Simply because it challenges my imagination.
If the theory really is true
Right now my cranial water molecules
Must be all a-tingle
And if you froze them
And looked at the crystals they formed—
You'd see what Wonder looks like.

A notable skeptic of this proposition
Has put up a million dollar reward
If the researcher in question here
Can prove his claims in a scientifically controlled,
Double blind test.
So far the money has gone unclaimed.

Some say the Statue of Liberty
Is a pagan symbol—
I say, "So what?"
Just means, for all practical purposes,
Its symbolic significance
Is not Christian or Islamic or Jewish.
Some say that makes it a "heathen" symbol,
Which is to say,
Not a religious symbol.
I find a certain comfort in that.
Others go even further,
Say the Statue's a symbol of Lucifer.
I laugh at them
And remind them
That Lucifer means "bearer of Light"
And that Light keeps company with Hope
And Tolerance
And Possibility!!
What sight could be more stirring
To human heart and mind
Than "Our Lady's" torch
Lifted to the sky?

(Interesting to wonder,
Why Liberty is so often portrayed
As a proud, strong Woman,
And not as a Colossal man with a sword—
A fact that Brightens me.)

A heart that
Goes out to the afflicted,
Wishes good for all,
Hopes for the best,
Yearns for the beautiful and true,
And loves life
Is praying as purely as it is possible to pray.

....

We've come so far—
From clubs and stones and spears
Applied from the ground
To "Fat Man" and "Little Boy"
Dropped from the sky;
From the walls of Jericho
To Hiroshima!
I cannot help but think
We're almost there.

....

He made the old argument
For the existence of God:
"If you came across a watch
In the middle of a vast desert,
Wouldn't you have to assume there was a Watchmaker?"
I tried not to look too indulgent
When I asked him back:
"And what would you have to assume
If, in a vast desert,
You came upon a Watchmaker instead?"

One day a little boy,
Unable to find meaning in his life,
Found in the wall of his considerable bewilderment
A round hole,
About the size of a hazelnut,
And desperate for meaning,
He pressed his eye to it
And peered through.
He must have seen something
Quite Marvelous,
For he spent much of the rest of his life
With his eye pressed to that hole.
One time I asked him about it,
And he told me
That he had only seen Something once,
That first time,
And that he goes back to it so often
Hoping desperately
That he might see it again.

....

She could not stand the sight of herself
And therefore kept a sheet over her mirror.
"Who would ever look twice at me," she grieved.
But she was an artist,
At least in her heart
And in her dreams,
And one day she decides
To take up brushes and paints
And sets to work
To canvas a "portrait" of her inner self.

And when she is finished
And stands back to look at what she's done,
She begins to cry:
"How could I be so Beautiful!!"
And she removes the sheet from the mirror
And hangs her portrait over it.
And then decides to paint another just like it
And hang it in her window
Facing the street.

....

The Night is dark,
Darker even than the mind of man,
And in the blackness of that great sweep of silent sky
An awesome shattering
Of broken glass and silvery dust,
And far beneath
That quiet spectacle
Of tiny glittering lights,
Throughout Germany and part of Austria,
Storm troopers and hooligans
Prowl the streets
With their hammers and their clubs and their stones—
Kristallnacht.

And there will be other Nights,
Darker nights than this,
Darker even than the heart of man—
Dachau, Buchenwald, Auschwitz,
Bergen Belsen, Treblinka, Sobibor...

Oh the beauty of restraints!
Of curtailments!
Of ethics!
And the rule of law!
We allow them to erode
To our great peril.
Too much freedom is a terrible thing.

Oh the ugliness of controls!
Of restrictions!
Of rigidity and regulation!
Of those who compel us!
We allow them to multiply
To our great peril.
Too much authority is a terrible thing.

....

My cat.
A plate glass window.
Birds just outside.
Feeding on seeds I put out.
How she used to crouch and chatter
In sheer excitement
When the birds were there.
Now she just lounges on the floor,
Watching with indifference
As they peck
And hop about
And scatter seeds.
I can't help but wonder
What I've done to her.

I went up to the door and knocked.
I had been told that if I knocked
It would be opened.
I knocked through the day
And through the night I knocked
Until finally my banging on the door
Had caused it to come ajar.
I hollered into the dark breach.
Said it was just me.
Could I come in?
Not a sound from inside.
I grew bold
And very gently pushed open the door,
Just enough to allow me to pass through.
It was dark inside and still
And I felt the presence
Of a profound vacancy—
Just then I heard a creaking
And turned to see the door swing open wide—
The wind, I thought,
But I took it as an invitation to leave.
On my way out,
For no accountable reason,
I turned and took one last look
Into that dark emptiness,
And at the top of the stairs,
Coming from beneath a closed door,
I thought I saw a slender edge of light.
"Probably just my imagination," I thought.
But when I left—
I left the door ajar.

A little girl is taken
To visit a Wonderland
And when she enters the Gate
She is amazed!
"Everything is so delicate and beautiful," she swoons.
But in the middle of the tour
She suddenly sits down on a bench
And begins to cry uncontrollably.
"Why are you crying?" asks the guide.
"Don't you understand," she sobs,
"This is all going to come to an end."
The guide looks a little puzzled.
"Yes, and for that reason
You should try to enjoy every moment you are here.
There is so much still to see,
And so much still to wonder at,"
Which only seems to make it worse for the little girl.
"Oh, I wish I hadn't come," she grieves,
And she pushes off the bench
And rushes to the exit gate,
Crying all the way.

....

She was a filthy derelict,
And smelled like something dead.
And she talked to herself
And drank from a bottle of cheap wine
And cursed anyone who came near,
And no one ever suspected
What her father started doing to her
When she was only eight years old.

Standing on the trap door,
He feels the warmth of the sun on his face
And the brush of a morning breeze
And he hears the bark of a distant dog
And the chatter of birds in the trees.
And his heart seems held in a calm embrace,
His mind at ease with it all,
As he waits with a strange and quiet grace—
For the sudden fall.

....

Jesus was not a political reformer
Nor a social reformer.
He was a reformer of individuals.
But to me,
More than anything else,
He was someone
Who reformed into a finer state
The very concept of God.
While he advanced that Great Work,
The work is not finished yet.

....

"As above so below."
So it has always been.
So it will always be.
Every so-called good and evil thing "below"
Issues from the mystery "above."
It's always "heaven" here on Earth
However otherwise it sometimes seems.

I wonder why I'm taking so much care
To see that these old locust posts
Are standing square
And why I fuss so much
To set the rails in just right—
Can hardly stand upright myself.
It seems a little on the foolish side
For one who's piled on so many years
To be out here so long in this October chill
Tending to a wooden fence that really doesn't need repair.
"You're holding up just fine," I say to it.
"No one would ever know you're just a little off.
Why should I care you lean a little this way or that
Or that your rails run a little up or down.
Maybe I look after you to give these crooked hands of mine
Some work to do
Or maybe just to pass the time of day.
No, I think it's something more than that, old Fence,
You're part of me,
And when some other in the years to come
Will chance to stand where I am standing now
And give your verticals a shake
To see if you're as steadfast as you look
And run his eye down your rough hewn limbs
To see if you're still true,
I want that other one to think of me—and to approve.
Maybe that is why I'm taking so much care.
Well, old Friend, I've done what I can do.
It's time to take my level up and go."

I came upon the Master
Sitting beside a dead body
Deep in meditation.
For a long time he sat there motionless like that,
And when he finally stood
I approached him and asked
If he were mourning
Or contemplating the mystery of Death.
The Master looked at me and smiled
And put his arm around my shoulder.
"Oh no, my young friend.
I was appreciating
The glorious Mystery of Life."

....

A man sits in his room,
Alone and despairing,
Slumped over,
Holding his head in his hands.
"I don't think I can go on," he mutters to himself.
Suddenly he hears a voice:
"Take my hand
And I will show you the way."
He looks around, bewildered.
Then stands,
Grumbles something about hearing things,
And leaves the room.

A man carefully selected
A number of iron bars
And gathered them about him
And with considerable skill
Welded them into
A place of secure incarceration.
And when he was finished,
He moved in
And was proud to call it home.
And after he had safely locked himself inside,
He tied the only key
Around the foot of a migrating bird
And set it free.

....

A knock on my door one winter night.
A woman with a petition.
She sees my cat.
Remarks how beautiful he is.
"He's old and failing," I sigh.
"I'm afraid I'm going to lose him soon."
Says she has some special medicines at home.
Thinks maybe they will help.
Tells me she'll come back with them
When she has finished canvassing her block.
Two hours later a knock on my door.
It's the woman again keeping her promise.
The medications—a powder and a gel.
She applies them with a cheerful hopefulness,
Her words an ointment and a balm.
And when she's finished ministering to him

She leaves me with the potions she has brought.
I thank her
And watch until she disappears into the night.
I never see her again.
My beautiful cat rallies
And lives for two more years!
And to this day I wonder
If those medications really worked?
Or was it her soft voice and gentle hands?
Or maybe just a chance effect?
I do know this:
In her unselfish willingness to minister to my cat—
She ministered to me.

....

The experience of Beauty
Is the only sacrament I take.
It's the simultaneous
Recognition of Self
In everything seen
And a recognition that everything seen
Is really Self—
It's the experience of Communion!
But the word for it that I like best
Is Recognition!
C'est un beau monde!

I've heard a rumor
That barnyard hens
Have formulated
The rudiments of religious thought,
Centered on the belief
That the farmer that scatters the seed
Is God.
The roosters, of course,
Naturally regard this view
With considerable skepticism.

Suppose it's true,
The Garden story.
We can't really undisobey God,
And we really can't uneat from the apple,
But we can give up this foolishness
That we know "Good" and "Evil."
If that doesn't get us back in the Garden
It should get us off our knees,
Get rid of a "damaging" "God,"
And get us out of the business
Of condemning people as heretics
And burning them at the stake.

....

Life is not a gift we get to keep.
It's loaned to us.
It makes no sense to some,
This gift of life that must be given back.
But is the only thing that does.

Middle of a frigid night.
A banging on your door,
A naked man,
Chalk-white with cold,
Shaking violently,
Face and body horribly scratched and bleeding.
Wild eyed.
Crazed.
Do you let him in?

Wandered off.
Morning.
Found in a nearby shed
Lying face down.
Arms out.
Frozen stiff.
Death opened the door for him.

A profanity
Or a blessing?

....

People who believe
In the coming of a new world order
Where we will all live together
In peace and harmony,
With liberty and justice for all,
Have taken the white cloth of their imagination,
Made a robe of it,
And placed it on the Dark shoulders of mankind.

War had come to the village where he lived,
And something worse than war.
And now he wanders in the woods,
Late into night,
Alone and terrified,
Trying to understand what had just happened.
He had been hiding behind a backyard tree
When they kicked in the door
And took his parents away.
Watched them pushed into the back of a heavy truck.
Heard it grumble down the road.
Now he's hiding in the woods
Fear taking him apart.
A little boy alone with his dying innocence.
Some hours pass.
Suddenly, machine gun fire, nearby.
He ducks into a thicket, cowers there.
A few more single shots ring out.
He flinches with each one,
As if each one has struck him.
Then he hears a truck start up.
A grinding gear,
And when the growling engine sound has died away,
A terrible, vile silence.
The smell of burned gunpowder finds where he is hiding.
It scares him. Tells a story he doesn't want to hear.
He waits. The darkness full of teeth and claws.
Finally he stands and chances out,
An awful dread upon him,
And makes his way through brooding trees
Toward where he heard the shooting come.

An openness ahead.
And when this little boy of only eight
Steps to the edge of that cleared place
And sees what he most fears to see,
He stops dead in his tracks,
And is murdered right there with the others.
Yes, It's true that he survived the war
And the obscenity of what he saw that night,
But the boy in him did not survive
And the man he turned into
Never came completely back to life.

....

We can look back
And we can look ahead,
But best of all:
We can "Look Around!"

....

A man was so successful in thinking outside the box
That he lost track of the man
Inside the box
Who was thinking outside the box.
It got so bad
That his friends became concerned
And told him that he had
To start learning how to think inside the box.

God says to a lump of nothingness:
I have a proposition for you:
I will make you into a living thing,
Give you the gift of Life,
The gift of My Life,
With all its joys and sorrows.
But there is one condition:
There will come a time
When I will ask you to return it to me,
And you must do so,
And when you do
You will become again just as you are now—
"But I'm nothing now."
Precisely.
What do you say?

....

Of all the creatures on the Earth
And in the sea and sky
It's only man
Who ponders life
And what it means to die.

....

She chose to steer her ship
Into the deep waters of the night sky
Where she was shipwrecked by the stars.
And though the vessel of her self was torn apart
Her spirit found a place to moor itself
Among the Harbor Lights.

The old Indian
Stoops out his wigwam.
The dog labors up and follows him outside
Where he prefers to sleep and keep a watch,
His muscles stiff and sore,
Like the old man's.
Wants to hear the treasure of the old man's voice,
Wants to feel his fingers
Scratch and ruffle up the top of his head.
The old man does not disappoint.
Then the old man totters off into the night,
Followed by the dog that totters after him.
The sky is black and over full of stars.
He does not venture far—
Stops.
Scrunches up the back of his neck
To take into his eyes
The sheer Wonder of the night sky.
Wants to feel the Great Mystery
Move through him.
The Wakan Tanka does not disappoint.
Then the old Indian looks down
Sees the dog looking up at him.
Bits of diamond in his eyes.
Offers his hand.
Feels the lick of his tongue.
"Twice blessed tonight," he says,
"The both of us. Twice blessed."
And the old dog gives a feeble bark,
And the two old friends
Turn and hobble back.

As he walked the dusty roads of Galilee,
Or the paths he took to get from place to place
Throughout Israel (Palestine),
I wonder how many times Jesus came upon
A lost or hungry dog
Or an injured dog,
Or one lame or sick.
I would guess that it was often,
So I find it strange and more than just a little sad
That in the gospel record
There is not a single instance that I know
Where Jesus ministered to dogs—
Or to any other animal than man.
And the few references to dogs I find
Are either callous or derogatory.

And except for his reference to the "Lilies of the Field"
I can't recall one other mention
Of Jesus being moved by
Anything Beautiful,
And I wonder how that can be.

....

God is Quarkiness—
Uncertainty.
Possibility.
Entanglement.
Irrationality.
If you want to meet God
Burglarize an Atom.

She was so self conscious
That she was conscious of herself being conscious of herself—
And when she was around others
She was conscious of them
Being conscious of her
And she was even conscious of herself
Being conscious
Of others being conscious of her!
She therefore lived her life
Trapped in a house of polished mirrors,
Completely unconscious
Of her Self.

....

Another I knew
Who was so lacking in self consciousness
That he was likely to forget his name,
And if he chanced to see his image
Reflected in the window of a shop
It seemed to take him by surprise
And he regarded it with curious disinterest,
And he went about in the world
As if he were invisible to others,
And they all but invisible to him,
Present among them
But seeming oddly absent.
"Elfin," some called him.
Others, "Strange."
I don't think he had any idea whatsoever
How utterly Beautiful he was.

You can only hate a thing if you don't understand it
And can only love a thing that you do.

....

Imagine:
Calamity on planet Earth.
All humanity has died—
You, the last surviving human being,
And you are in your final time.
It's hard enough
To face the last hour of your own personal life,
But what thoughts occur,
What feelings come,
As humanity prepares to take its final breath,
As the human heart and mind
Is about to vanish from this once garden place?
All that men and women ever thought and hoped
And ever wondered or dared or dreamed
Is about to die with you...

And now here you are,
Late into night
Alone in all the world,
Lying on the ground, unable to move,
Gazing up into a welkin full of stars.
Your eyes heavy.
You try but cannot keep them open.
You feel your final tears roll down your cheeks.
Then your eyes fall closed
As the last of human kind perishes from the Earth.

A single copper penny.
More than 20,000,000,000,000,000,000,000 copper atoms!!
Each atom: 29 protons, 29 electrons, 3 neutrons.
(Not to mention all the quarks
Cavorting in the protons and neutrons
And behaving in the most confounding ways),
Yet if a hundred million Absolutely identical copper pennies
Are flipped into the air,
In exactly the same way,
Under exactly the same conditions,
Starting with the same side up,
They will all come down with exactly the same result:
All heads or all tails—
Completely uninfluenced by all the subatomic goblins
Ghosting about inside.
If I am wrong about this
It is likely I am wrong about everything—
Which of course I may be—and probably am.

....

If there's a goblin loose
In your house
That you can't access with your senses,
And that goblin has no ability
To interact with your material reality,
What possible difference can it make to you?
Especially if you don't know it's there—
But even if you do?

Inside every mind
Is a safe that most of us
Can crack with relative ease,
And inside that safe
Is a succession of smaller and smaller safes,
Each one more difficult to break into
And each containing treasures of increasing value.
And in the last and smallest safe of all
The very secret of Being is kept—
The problem is
It can only be opened from the inside.

....

Given one Big Bang,
Why not another?
Why not a Garden of expanding Universes?
Room enough in infinite space
For as many as we can imagine.
(I suppose we can only imagine such a thing,
Since how would we ever know?)
But having imagined it,
Maybe "our" Cosmos
Just blossoms out into
A vast field of blossoming Others,
And the escaped energy of those
That have "blossomed out"—
Comes together in a kind of nursery
Of orphaned light
Or are gathered up by gigantic singularities
Where other Cosmic eggs are hatched
And other "men" and "gods" are born!

Next time you get caught up in your own personal celebrity,
Get in touch with the chicken-wire fabric of your cranium
And go soak your papier-mâché head
In a bucket of warm water.

....

Nature
Can be a nurturing mother,
Embracing and facilitating life,
Or a ruthless purveyor of death and devastation.
You could say that Nature
Is careless of what she does—
And I think it's true she does not care:
Spring showers do not fall with kind intent
Nor does a raging volcano
Have an ax to grind.

....

Such an Earth and Sea and Sky this was!
So much Beauty and Diversity!
And so much Wonder!
With so much possibility
And so much promise!
How did it ever come to pass
We ended up *On the Beach?*
The saddest thing of all
Is not that we didn't know
What would happen if...
But that we did!!!
(I think maybe the movie made this point??)

Master, is the Cosmos conscious of itself?
"Are you conscious of the Cosmos?"
Well, yes, to the extent I'm able, I am.
"Do you come to me today with any other questions?"

Master, is the Cosmos conscious of me?
"Not in the way you are conscious of it—or of yourself."
In what way then?
"As a clay pot is conscious of the Potter."
Is a clay pot conscious of the potter then?
"Not in the way the Potter is conscious of the pot."

Master, did the Cosmos evolve us to be conscious of it?
"Do you think the Cosmos has a need to be noticed?"
I don't know, Master, but it seems natural that it would?
"It seems natural that a man would think that."

Master, what happens after I die?
"What happened before you were born?"
How could I possibly know that, Master?
"Thank you. You have served me well."

Why is there evil in the world, Master?
"Why is there a dragon in the garden?"
But Master, there is no dragon in the garden.
"How quickly you learn."

Why was I born, Master?
"You think you were born for some reason then?"
Well, if I wasn't born for a reason why was I born?
Why do you smile, Master?

Master, why do you contemplate the Cosmos so much?
  "You will not misunderstand me?"
I will try not to, Master.
  "Because I am Self absorbed."

Master, is the Cosmos beautiful to you?
  "I find nothing in it that is ugly."
Does that mean you find it beautiful?
  "It means I find it as it IS."

....

When all things have occurred
That can occur
Can it really be said
That anything occurred at all??
When all that IS becomes annihilate
Won't it be exactly
As if nothing ever was?

....

From Stardust to Stardust

....

We leave our sticky snares behind
And come with trusting heart and mind
To see what visions might appear
And find what treasures we might find.
"Weaving spiders come not here." (W.S.)

I came across a "shield" bug today
About eye level on the glass of my storm door,
Just sitting there alone and still,
Perhaps invited by a smattering of winter sun.
Her tiny feet no doubt could tell how cold it was outside,
But still it seemed to me she wanted out,
Though why she would want out I couldn't guess
As being out for very long this frigid day
Would mean the end of her
(Though prospects for her staying here inside with me
Seemed just as grim).
My heart goes out to any creature trapped,
And having given it some thought
I got her in my hand,
Pushed out the door,
And gently placed her on the Christmas wreath that hung out-
side,
A fresh arrange of Norway spruce.

I had some things to do that took me from the house,
And on that errand out I worried what I'd done,
And hoped the sun would cover my mistake,
And when an hour later I returned
I went to see if I could find her on the wreath,
And there she was just as I left her there,
A delicate design of brown on sprucy green,
But it appeared the cold had done her in
As she lay turned upon her side,
Her tiny limbs drawn up in that familiar pose
That dead things take.
I gently tipped her in my hand

And took her back inside.
"Maybe you'll revive once you warm up," I thought.
But she looked quite intent on staying dead.
And after some time watching her not move
I placed her body upright on the mantle top,
As much as that was possible to do
With legs all folded up like that,
And left her slightly tilted there
While I went off to do some other chores.

Perhaps another hour passed
Before I thought to check on her,
And what a rush of joy and what relief to me
To find that she was now positioned
Squarely on her feet,
And though not moving much,
At least alive and moving some!
"What now to do with you now you've thawed out?"
I wondered to myself out loud.
And then I saw the bright poinsettia
Potted on the table near the door.
"So that's how you got in!
If I had noticed that before
I never would have set you out,"
And so I gentled her into my hand again,
Placed her in the potted earth
And let her be.

Two days go by
Before I risk another look,
And after some time poking through the brightly petaled plant

Continued

I spot her standing upside down
Nonchalantly feeding on a leaf.
I'm sure she doesn't know
What we have put each other through,
And just as well:
The old man knows—
Which is enough.

....

The cloistered monk
Denies himself the pleasures of this world
Preferring rather to please "God,"
I guess believing that "God"
Has a need to be made happy
And that need can only be satisfied
By unhappy men,
Or by men made happy
By foregoing the pleasures of this world
In order to make "Him" happy.

....

Even God must yield to the Inevitable.

....

Two brick walls facing each other.
Each one has a mouth
But neither has ears.
If they speak their minds
They are fools.

Alaska.
Over twenty years ago
An oil spill
A beautiful bald eagle,
Rescued, cleaned, banded, released.
Twenty hears later.
Attracted to refuse from the fishing boats
Alights on a live wire of a utility pole.
Electrocuted.
Falls in a heap
Into a mound of dirty snow.

....

I come upon a brooding man
And ask what troubles him.
"I am unable to keep
From thinking about the Dark Ages," he glooms.
When I show my dismay
An ask him why such a period of time
Consigned now to the distant past
Should anguish him so much,
He looks up at me forlornly and replies,
"I am not thinking of the Dark Ages of the past
But of the Dark Age of the present—
And the Darker Age to come."

....

He fought his fate
(Not knowing that it was his fate to fight his fate.)
And "willed" his way to where his fate awaited him.

When my lungs exhale for the last time
And my body goes limp,
My final thought
Will not be of any earthly thing
Or any thought of heaven or hell—
But simply what has
Enchanted me my entire life—
The profound Mystery of Being.

....

Saintly old woman dies,
Survived by husband who worshipped her
And a loving daughter.
While going through her mother's things
The daughter
Discovers a bundle of letters
Carefully hidden away
Revealing that the saintly mother,
For most of her married life,
Had a secret lover.
The daughter believes strongly
That "The truth will set you free,"
And three weeks after the mother is buried,
While grief still rends her father's heart,
The loving daughter
Sits down with him,
And though it is very hard for her to do,
She puts the letters in his lap
And sets her father "free."

On his uncertain wanderings
Through the mapless way of his life
He came upon one fork in the road after another
And each time made a deliberate choice
To go this way or that,
And when the trails diminished
And became no trail at all
He pressed into the uncharted wilderness,
And picked a ragged course
Through the density of trees
Till at length,
As the day was about to turn into night,
He chanced upon a clearing
Where, to his astonishment,
He found a small rustic Inn,
And when he entered the lodging place
He was warmly greeted by the Innkeeper:
"Welcome, Good Sir.
Come in! Come in!
We've been expecting you!"

. . . .

Two things,
Both occurring in such great abundance
That the mind and sensibilities of man
Are not able to process their excess:
The overwhelming suffering taking place in the world,
And the exquisite Beauty that everywhere abounds!

When I asked the true believer
How he could be so certain about his beliefs,
He took me a little by surprise by answering strongly,
I don't really believe—
I KNOW!!
And when I asked him
How he could "know" what can only be believed
He smiled knowingly and said,
"First you have to believe—
Have to WANT to believe—
And then you have to act
AS IF what you want to believe is actually true,
And after awhile it will be,
And then you'll KNOW."
I looked at him doubtfully,
Entertaining the image of a horse
Nudging the cart along from behind,
Then imagining a frog
Going to sleep every night
Muttering to himself
"I am a prince, I am a Prince, I am a Prince"
And waking up one morning
Wearing a purple robe.

....

If Man is a Cosmic "self" portrait,
We can only hope it's a "work in progress."

From the beginning
The Cosmos began evolving.
Ten Billion years later—planet Earth,
Where the chemistry of "Life" begins.
And after four billion years
Of biological evolution—
Contemplative man!!
(How patient the evolutionary process!)
My question Is:
Was this outcome
"Contemplated" by the Cosmos
Or just an inevitable consequence—
And does it make a difference which?

....

Possibility is a closed door that isn't locked;
certainty isn't even a door.

....

Every night
As I close my eyes
And lay me down to sleep
I open the doors of my mind as wide as I can,
And fasten them open,
Not only to let any thing "out there" in
But to let anything in "here" out.
It's what I do
Instead of pray.

When she was a child
She wanted one thing
More than anything else in the world.
More than milk and cookies
More than pretty clothes
More than playing with her friends—
More than anything!
And did everything she could to get it,
But never knew it
Because it was never shown—
Her father's affection.

....

Paris,
Velodrome d'Hiver (Vel' D'Hiv'),
July 16 & 17, 1942
French gendarmes
(Under Nazi command)
"Roundup" over 8,000 Jews,
Pack them in the sweltering Vel' d'Hiv,
More women than men,
More children than men and women combined—
So many bewildered and terrified little children—
Detain them there for six days in atrocious conditions,
Herd them into cattle cars,
And rail them off to Auschwitz…
The Roundup code name:
"Operation Spring Breeze."
Zakhor. Al Tichkah.

It cannot be
That space itself goes on forever,
And yet it does,
And if it does not
Then what does it come up against?
It cannot be
That the energy of the Cosmos
Was always present in some "form" or another.
And yet it was,
And if it wasn't,
Where did it come from?
(The Big Bang Theory
Is not an answer but another question.)
The Prime Questions are confounding,
Unanswerable—
Blind spots in the eye of human rationality.
And what they show us
Is not only that we don't know it all
But that the All
May be unknowable—
And when you think about it
How "Wonderful" is that!!"

....

If you believe only what you see,
You are partially blind.
And if you believe everything you see,
You are a fool.

When a grieving man,
Having convicted himself
And in the process of "serving time,"
Wails at the Master,
"Even God could not forgive me
The hideous things I've done!"
The Master allows some time to pass
Before he calmly tells the grieving man,
"God has no need to forgive."

....

When I was a little boy—
Maybe seven or eight years old—
I killed a squirrel with a rock.
I was horrified at what I'd done—
And came back later to see
If maybe I'd just knocked it out,
Hoping against hope
That it had come to
And was up in a tree somewhere
Twitching its tail in an effort to clear its head,
But there it lay
Just as dead as I left it.
It's been over sixty years now
Since I buried it in my heart,
And I can't tell you how many times
I still visit the "grave."

I wonder if the truth isn't really this simple:
That there is an explanation for everything,
(Which we may or may not ever learn—
Or even be able to learn, for that matter)
But there is no reason for anything.
Everything is theoretically understandable in terms
Of how it came to be or to pass,
But there is no why in terms of intention or purpose.
We can explain the collapse of a bridge, for instance,
The conditions that caused it to collapse,
But it didn't collapse "for a reason,"
As a result of some supernatural or cosmic intention.
Of course this gets a little dicey for me
Since I think everything happens inevitably,
Exactly as it must,
And if that is so,
Then you could make a case
That that is precisely Cosmic "intention,"
Especially if you were very expansive
In your definition of "intention."
I wonder if there is really a difference
Between saying that the Cosmos
"Intends" everything to happen just as it does,
And that everything happens just as it does
Because it could not happen in any other way.

. . . .

Everything makes sense
When everything makes sense,
But when nothing makes sense anymore,
What makes sense then?

Set up a lawn chair on the dusty Moon.
Arrange it to face a "full Earth."
Sit back and gaze at that gleaming thing,
That beautiful marble out there,
Suspended in the blackness of boundless space,
The black behind it all sifted with tiny points of light.
Do not take your eyes from it.
Behold it!
Reflect on its 4.5 billion years of geologic history,
Of the long evolution of life,
Of the advent of man on it,
So soon ago!
So soon ago
That the whole history of homo sapiens
Is like a current event,
Which is passing even as it occurs.
How all but imaginary
The race of man!
And you are there on it,
There on that magic planetary place—
Yet at this very moment siting in this webbed chair,
Here in this rocky lunar dust.
You are out there on that luminous biosphere,
Thinking what you think, feeling what you feel,
Perhaps this very moment
Looking up,
Taken out of yourself
By that small bright pearl "up there"
That luster in the sky that has observed so much
And yet has seen nothing at all.
If you could leap and bound ahead through time,

You'd see the round whiteness of it recede
Till it gets lost in the distant suns of other worlds
And watch the stars themselves wink out one by one
Till only the immensity of black remains.
But for now there's the weight of yourself in the lawn chair
And that lovely round of Earth and sea out there
Swirled with wispy streaks of white and grey,
And you down there on it looking up
Lost in the profound enormity of space—
Caught in a blink of imaginary time.

....

Papa, when people say they "believe"—
You know, like in God
And heaven and stuff like that,
Is that the same thing as "making believe"?

....

Lots of ugly four-letter words:
I could list them all,
But I'm thinking of just one—
The ugliest, most sinister,
Most terrifying and disturbing,
Most ominous and foreboding of them all,
Hate!
I'm not sure,
But I think of all the creatures on the Earth
Only we "sapiens" do it—
And mostly to each other.

It is quite possible to love too much—
And to be loved too much—
For love is an art
And as such it is both a liberty—
And a discipline.
Uncontrolled or controlled too much
It can turn on itself
And devour both the lover—
And the loved.

....

Ethics emerged naturally enough
In primitive clans and tribes:
A growl and a cuff
Determined what was "wrong"
And a smile and a grunt of approval
What was "right."
No doubt clans had a secular Code of conduct—
Clan rules.
Morality was only established later
When somebody got the dim idea
That a great Judgmental Male
Lived up in the stars somewhere
Who was watching and taking notes,
And the "tribal rules"
Became the "Ten Commandments."
Right and wrong
Became Good and Evil,
And ever since we poor creatures
Have had to fear not only the back of a hand—
But the wrath of God!

Sitting by the side of the road,
Taking in the natural beauty of the world
And enjoying the wonder of just being alive,
I notice a man approaching in considerable haste.
When he gets to me he stops,
Bends forward at the waist,
Puts his hands on his knees,
And gasps for breath.
And when I ask if he's all right,
He raises a hand and nods that he is okay.
Then straightens up,
Takes a deep breath,
And speeds on down the road—
In "pursuit of happiness."

....

Remote "Pacific" Isle,
Densely covered with Emerald Green Palms,
Discovered by early Polynesian voyagers
Who, for many centuries, flourished there...
Then all but vanished,
But not without a trace,
Leaving behind hundreds
Of brooding monolithic Moai
Facing the sea,
Backs turned
On the ruined Island Paradise.

A strand of barbed wire
Strung across a cleared expanse of land,
Perhaps to mark a property line.
Over seventy years later
An old man on an excursion through the woods
Sees a strange slight:
A large Beech tree
With a fragment of twisted wire,
Sticking out of each side,
All but eaten away by rust.
He stops to wonder at it.
He can imagine a young sapling
Pressing up alongside it,
Many long years ago,
Maybe right against a sharp barb,
And over the years growing around it,
Absorbing it into itself.
He can imagine that sharp barb
Now lodged in the heartwood of the aging tree—
And that contemplative thought
Is more a personal recollection
Than the old man is willing to concede.

....

To me prayer is not so much talking to "God"
As just "listening."
I shouldn't say "just"
Because true listening
Requires a near-perfect discipline,
Is an act of supreme "self" control.

"Meaning" is something we impose on our "reality,"
And "value" is something we assign.
Without us what does anything mean?
Without us, not even "God" makes any sense.
(Even with us the sense is hard to come by)
Actually, there is meaning and value in the Cosmos—
Even here in our own biosphere—
But that meaning and value
Is independent of and oblivious to
Our own personal conceits.

....

When I consider the question:
"Am I my brother's keeper?"
I am first moved to ask myself,
"Would I want to be kept by my brother?"
And of course the answer is
That I would not,
For it seems to me
There is very little difference
Between keeping a brother
And keeping a slave—
Or keeping a pet.
Any such keeping is a theft
Not only from the keeper—
But from the kept!
It is an exploitation,
And when a government is predicated on such a notion
It is a tyranny.

After my dad had abandoned us,
My mother,
Who was made of pretty stern stuff,
Was left with four children
To raise by herself.
Refusing any form of public assistance,
She rolled up her sleeves,
Steeled herself
And bravely took on
What life had placed in front of her.
We lived in a house she rented
From my dad's father,
And for the first year,
With little to no help from my absent father,
She was not able to pay the rent.
My grandfather allowed us to stay in the house—
My mother promising to pay the arrears to him
When she was able.
She found work,
Learned the hard lessons of frugality and sacrifice,
Put food on our table and clothes on our back,
Scrimped and saved what little she could—
And after that first year
Began paying our monthly rent.
Two years later,
From her meager earnings,
She had put enough money aside
To settle her debt with my grandfather.
I like to think he offered to forgive it
And that my mother wouldn't hear of it.
I remember thinking at the time

What she could have done for us
With all that money—
Which was nothing to him,
But a small fortune to us—
And it was not until years later
That I realized how much she did do for us—
By paying it back.
(Maybe my grandfather's wisdom
Tutored his charitable instincts.
Maybe he knew what price my mother would pay
If he had refused her recompense.
Whatever his intention,
He let my mother keep something
Far more precious
Than the stack of bills she placed in his hand,
And she passed that something on to us.)

....

He stretched a canvas in his mind
And with a rhapsody of colors
Painted a picture
Of the world
As he imagined it could be,
And when he had finished
He stepped back
And looked at it,
And for a few short moments
Was transported out of himself—
And then he dropped to his knees
And wept himself to death.

Imagine an actor in a play
Who gets so caught up in his part
That he becomes the character he's playing,
And his scripted words
Become spontaneous,
And his directed actions
Become naturally occurring,
And the others in the play
Become real to him...
In short, he and his world become delusional—
Which is to say his delusional world
Becomes real.
And as it is for him;
So it is for us all.

....

"Why do you believe things
That are –well—unbelievable?"
Asked one of another.
The other came back,
"First of all nothing is unbelievable;
But to answer directly,
In the absence of any evidence
I believe what comforts me,
And I wonder why you choose not to believe such things."
"I guess because I am comfortable
With the truths
That make you uncomfortable."

In a delusional world.
The most delusional
Have an adaptive advantage
Over those who see things as they are,
Just as in a madhouse
The truly demented
Are more comfortably situated
Than those who are sane.

....

A delicate moth—
Gossamer,
Sublimely iridescent wings,
Struggling in a most exquisite snare.
The spider,
Itself a creature of intricate and sublime design,
Bearing down on her.
With keen intent.
Such is the nature of nature—
And of "super nature!"

....

I don't really believe in "God"—
Not as something separate from the Cosmos Itself,
Certainly not as some kind of spiritual entity
Modeled after a "perfect" man.
I think of "God" AS the Cosmos Itself,
Perfect as it IS.

I completely reject
The silly concept of a "Chosen People,"
The Jews "chosen" because they have the Torah
And the promise of a Messiah,
The Moslems because they have Mohammed,
The Christians, Jesus etc.
They all think that "God" favored them
"Chose" them to speak to,
To make "his" children,
Now and forever—
But not the "others."
"To hell with them."
What a narrow and disparaging view of "God!"
Out of their own smallness
They have made a small god.
Out of their own provincial conceit
They have created a "God"
In the flawed image of themselves!

....

Her mind was so open,
Her heart so large,
Her compassion so complete,
She lived in perpetual commiseration
With all suffering creatures.
Happiness therefore
Was impossible for her.
"A God of infinite Love," she thought,
Must know a constant and unspeakable Sorrow."
And thinking that
She began to commiserate with God.

Too much smog!
Too much diffusion of incandescent light!
(Too much diffusion of inner light)
Too long the bad habit
Of not bunching up the back of our neck on a dark night
To Wonder the Stars.

....

If the essence of the Cosmos is not rational
Then is it rational
To "believe" you can reason out its essence?

....

I'm thinking about the Speed of Gravity and wondering
If gravity even has speed? Is it anything like Light?
Does the gravity of the Sun, for example,
Travel out from the Sun to reach, say, the Earth?
(And the gravity of Earth to the Sun?)
If it does, then I wonder this:
If the Sun suddenly ceased to be,
How long would it take before the Earth
Would be set free from its influence?
(Or put the other way:
If the Sun instantly came into being,
Would an "earth" be instantly attracted to it?
Or would it take "time" for the Sun's pull to reach the Earth?)
I have talked to some who "know" the answer,
But the answer that they give is "questionable."

I watch a wee spider crawling up a wall,
I Wonder, wee wonder,
What it is you Wonder
In that wee mind of yours—
Or if you Wonder anything at all.

....

Every event in the Cosmos—
From stellar nurseries
To colliding galaxies,
From the lighting of a Christmas candle
To the incendiary bombing of Dresden—
Is an "Act of God."

....

The old lady hobbled to a wooden chair,
Feeling a little like the stiff chair herself,
(Though not sure-footed, she thought,
And not straight-backed, like the chair)
And slowly got herself sat down.
She felt brown inside and dried out
And used up.
"What use am I?" she sighed.
"Who would miss me if I slept away this night?"
And then she thought of the Violets
In the east window.
"They would miss me," she thought,
And that thought watered her.

Two men approached our gathering,
One handsome and distinguished,
The other something of a toad.
The man of obvious quality
Asked if we would be kind enough
To give him a brief audience
(He had tidings to impart of great import),
Which we did.
As he articulated his wisdom,
I noticed that the toad stood by,
Silent and unattending,
Seeming to mind his own Internal Wonderings.
When our distinguished guest
Had concluded his presentation
He thanked us,
Politely gave us a nod,
And the two men departed.
I could not help to observe to the others:
"One of those men was surely wise,
And the other surely a fool."

....

At a metropolitan zoo
A menacing beast
Paws at the heavy glass barrier
Separating a man from a huge lion.
Then the menacing beast
Sticks out his tongue,
Makes an obscene gesture
And struts away
Laughing like a fool.

When I was a little boy
I used to go into my mother's bedroom,
To lift the lid of an old music box
That sat on her dressing table.
I loved the beautiful tune it played.
How many times over the years that tune
Has tinkled in my head,
Yet I never heard the contrapuntal.
It wasn't until many years later
That I heard the haunting counterpoint for the first time.
How astonished I was!!
Now when I lift the lid
And hear the tines strike out the tune,
I hear first the haunting background strain.
It has become the melody in my mind!
And I can't help but wonder if the ordinary "melody" of Life
Doesn't have an extraordinary "harmony"
Which goes unnoticed by most of us.

....

Biblically speaking,
the original sin was an act of disobedience to God,
But it's my belief that the original "sin" is believing that we
CAN disobey God.
The deepest wisdom that I know
Is founded on the virtually inconceivable notion,
With all its profound implications,
That it is impossible to disobey "God"!

Poland, midwinter.
The night, bitter cold.
Steam rises from a heap of dead bodies
Stacked in a yard,
Near the crematorium.
In her extremity, a young girl
Has wandered from her wooden ghetto
And climbed atop the horrible pile
In search of warmth.
She curls up into a final resting place
And shivers herself to death.
Overhead,
Remote and indifferent,
A multitude of stars
Shimmer in the black sky.

....

We all know it is not possible to alter the past,
But here's the astonishing thing:
Neither is it possible to alter the future!!

....

I come upon Despair slumped on a park bench,
His eyes lifeless,
His heart a wasted thing.
In his lap he holds a cardboard sign,
Crudely scrawled on it, these words:
"I was never born."

I sit down next to a woman at a bar.
She looks up from her drink,
And when our eyes meet in the mirror,
She brightens,
Then turns to me and smiles:
"I've been waiting for such a long time."
"I'm sorry," I said.
"Do I know you?"
The smile slides from her face.
As she looks back down at her drink:
"I wish somebody did."

....

A despairing man stands on the edge of a bridge,
Arms out, fingers loosely resting on the rail.
"God has forsaken me," he moans.
Suddenly he hears a bicycle rattle to a stop
And a small voice ask,
"Hey, Mister. I don't mean to bother ya,
But the chain's come off my bike,
And I was wonderin' if you could give me a hand with it."

....

I don't think the Cosmic Mind
Has a memory or an imagination.
It is too preoccupied processing the ever-evolving Present
To have "time" to look back
Or any prompting to look forward.

When a true believer asks me about God,
I open my heart and mind to him
And when I tell him of
The Oneness I know
And the Harmony I experience
When I commune with the All of Everything,
Tears come to my eyes
And I am overwhelmed.
The true believer
Listens indulgently,
And it doesn't bother me
That tonight he will pray for my "immortal soul."

....

A man stands on the corner.
He carries a sign which says,
"The Beginning is Near."

....

Is there a greater "blasphemy"
A more offensive idolatry—
Than the turning of an animal into God,
Be it a golden calf—or a man!

....

If I had to shoot a wild animal
In order to keep from starving to death,
I think it would be a lucky day
For the wild animal.

When someone asked me once:
"If the Cosmos that you love
Had a face,
And after your death
You came to look upon that face,
What expression would you expect to see?"
"I wouldn't expect to see any expression whatsoever," I replied.
But if I had to imagine such a thing,
Maybe I would say,
A look of One Accord."

....

If you want to know what "god" is like,
You might do well to closely examine
What we call "acts of God."

....

I spy a Barred Owl in the park today,
Roosting in a high tree.
I draw near and lift my eyes to him.
"What a solitary stillness you are!" I say.
He looks down and winks one eye at me.

....

I sometimes wonder
If our personal need to be valued and embraced
By something larger and beyond ourselves
Isn't prompted by something larger and beyond ourselves
That needs to be valued and embraced.

Here lies the crumpled remains
Of Blandina Drake
Who got to the end of her rope
And held on—
For over sixty years!
In the end
It wasn't her strength that failed,
But the rope.

....

The little boy
Crawled into bed,
Said his prayers,
And with the help of the Sandman,
Fell asleep.
And how he Dreamed!
When he awoke
He was dismayed to discover
That he had dreamed himself into an old man.

....

Don Quixote was decrepit
And delusional
And pathetic,
But because he was True
To the Bright Star that hung in his Sky—
He was Beautiful!!
That's the main thing now, isn't it—
To be "Truly" Beautiful.

Every morning the Sparrows
Congregate in the Lilac bush
Growing just outside my kitchen window,
Waiting for me to come with the seeds,
Many positioned so they can watch me
Moving about inside,
But what amuses me
Is that after the feeder is filled
And I have returned to my seat at the table near the window,
I notice that this one Sparrow
Has not joined in the melee
Taking place around the seeds,
But stands his slanted twig
And regards me Wonderingly,
Tilting his head a little to one side,
As if trying to ponder me out—
Or maybe endeavoring to put together
The rudiments of a theology.

....

I believe that at the bottom of every heart,
Situated in a little depression there,
Is a leaden basin
Filled with unshed tears.
For most of us the basin catches the condensation
From our personal sorrows,
But others, I think
Have a basin of tears
Fed from some deep primordial spring.)

When I was a little boy
I had an imaginary friend.
And the really strange thing is
He had one too—
Which was me.
And all these many years later,
I'm still not sure
That he was imaginary,
And all these many years later
I am equally uncertain
That I became real.

....

A young woman
Draws near the Master
And settles herself in front of him,
And when she asks,
"Master is there life for us after we die?"
The Master remains motionless
Looking at his hands folded in his lap.
For some long moments
He does not speak.
At length he looks up at her,
Smiles reassuringly,
And says only,
"The day is quite beautiful,
Don't you think?
Will you excuse me now?"

The little girl
Tugged her mother out the door
And towed her into the front yard.
"Hurry, Mom, Oh please hurry!"
She pointed to the sky:
"See! See!"
Looking up,
There in the blue of it,
The mother saw a narrow mark of cloud.
"I made it, Mommy. I made it!"
In the little girls' hand—
A blunt piece of white chalk.

....

I talked to a lady once
Who told me she never cried
Because she was afraid
That once she started
She would never be able to stop.

....

I come upon an Adept gazing into a crystal ball.
I ask him what he sees,
He looks up at me
But does not speak.
However I notice
A Vacancy in his eyes.

"Excuse me, Sir,
I can't help but notice that you never laugh;
Does nothing amuse you?"
The man looks at me
And replies darkly,
"Well, my curious friend,
The obvious answer is
That I find nothing funny,
But the truth is—
I find everything funny,
And that's kind of sad,
Don't you think?"

. . . .

I harken to many of the teachings of the Jewish Rabbi
And none more than when Peter comes to him and asks,
"Lord, how oft shall my brother sin against me
And I forgive him?
Till seven times?"
And Jesus looks deep into Peter's eyes and answers,
"I say not unto thee, until seven times;
But until seventy times seven."
But I cannot harken to the affirmations of the Apostles' Creed,
Especially the part that declares
That the Jewish Rabbi
"Will come again to judge the quick and the dead."
What a thing to say!!
Can anyone imagine the Gentle Rabbi
Casting the stone of final judgment!!

When I come upon an unhappy woman
I stop and ask her why she is so downcast.
And when she looks up at me
I can see a profound melancholy in her eyes.
"Because there is so little in me to admire."
"But we are all flawed,"
I say to comfort her.
"Yes, but you don't understand:
Of the people I have known in my life
I am the most admirable of them all."

....

What does it profit a man
If he frees himself from the chains that bind him
Only to bind himself in a new set of chains?

....

When a woman comes to the Master
And cries out to him:
"Oh, Master, you've got to help me.
I am near ruin.
I can no longer bear the endless injustices of this world,
The undeserved suffering that seems to exist everywhere?
What can I do?
Please, Master, tell me,
What can I do?"
The Master thoughtfully considers her question
Then answers evenly,
"Try to be more like God."

Walking down the road of life one day
I observe another
Approaching me.
I am surprised to see that he is wrapped in chains
But even more perplexed to note
That he is smiling broadly
And whistling a merry tune.
"Excuse me, Sir,
But how is it you are so lighthearted
Wrapped as you are in heavy chains?"
"I'm sorry, my good man,
But I have no idea what you are talking about."
And lifting his arms as best he can, he says,
"Do you see any chains on me?"
I am at a loss for words
And watch as he smiles at me in wonderment,
Gives his head a little shake,
Then continues whistling on his way,
Accompanied by the rattle of his chains.

....

A child who was born in the dark
And grew up in in the dark
And has only known the dark,
Would be blinded by the Light,
Would hide his eyes and turn away
From any approaching with a Light.

The quantum world is amoral
The Cosmos at large is amoral
And the Earth,
And everything upon the Earth is amoral—
Except man—
Who thinks he knows better.

....

I heard somewhere once
That "undeserved suffering is redemptive."
I'm trying to understand what that means.
I guess it's based on the assumption
That we are all under judgment from above,
And that if we don't otherwise qualify for redemption,
But have suffered enough unjustly in this world,
We are spared from any judgment in the next.
Is that what it means?
And if there's no judgment in the next??
Then the statement is outrageous!

....

I stood in the Present and looked back
And I saw the horrific Past looking at me,
And the figure gestured to me not to return;
And I looked ahead
And saw the Future some little way ahead
Gesturing, "Turn back, turn back!"

We can inflate our personal insignificance
To such an extent
That we come to believe,
Not only that the Cosmos is mindful of us,
But that we are the apple of the Cosmic Eye!!

....

Death is just the process of dispersing
Our atomic constituents
Back where they came from,
And no doubt back where they belong—
Where they will not be judged,
But utilized.

....

When she said with quiet assurance,
"No one can hurt you
Unless you let them,"
I thought that might be true for some few of us
Who have turned ourselves into a stone Buddha,
Or some few others of us
Who have fitted ourselves out in a suit of heavy armor,
But surely she could not be thinking
Of the 800,000 Tutsi civilians in Rwanda,
Who, not many years ago,
In "one hundred days of terror,"
Were hacked to death by machete-wielding Hutus
Intent on eliminating the "cockroaches."

One day from my back window
My beautiful cat, Zoey,
Spotted a handsome male cat prowling
About in the yard,
The sun gleaming off his coat,
His shoulder muscles bunching as he walked.
How she swooned for him, my Zoey!
I think it was love at first sight.
Anyway, the male prowler wandered off
And never to my knowledge
Passed this way again.
It's been many years since that day
And still my Zoey
Keeps a frequent vigil at that window.
Oh I know she likely never gave that cat another thought,
But I can't help but think
That male rover still prowls her dreams
And that she lives in Hope
That some day he'll come back again.

....

Perhaps when man became self conscious
He also became able to observe himself from outside of himself,
And then was able to imagine that he was being observed
By a Being superior to himself
That like himself could get angry and violent.
I wonder if that might be when mankind
First started to think about and fear
The "wrath of God."

I understand that the great apes
Have 96% of the same genetic makeup as man—
But I don't' hold that against them.

....

I have wondered this:
If Adam and Eve
Didn't know good from evil—
What they should and shouldn't do—
Until after they had eaten the fruit
From the tree of knowledge,
How did they know that they should obey God
And that it was wrong to do what
They were told not to do?

....

Sometimes when I step out of the house
At the break of a new day
I am so struck by the sudden freshness of it
And the beauty and the goodness and the truthfulness of it,
I can't keep my heart
From breaking out of my chest
And chasing about through the wet morning grass,
And for a few moments
I forget what I know about the menace
That lurks in that exhilarating heart.

There is an answer to the question,
"Why me?"
But it has nothing to do with you.

....

And I have this question regarding the 2nd Creation Story:
Were Adam and Eve evicted from the Garden
As punishment for disobeying God (the Gods)
By eating from the tree of knowledge?
Or were they expelled
Because they had become God-like
After eating the forbidden fruit,
And God (the Gods) didn't want them
To stay in the Garden
Where they would surely eat of the Tree of Life
And become immortal like "them" ("one of Us").

Could it be that the gods themselves
Were burdened by the wisdom of their moral knowing,
And didn't want to visit that eternal burden
On their human creation?
Or were they just protecting
Their dominion in the heavenly realm?

(Also: Since Adam and Eve were not forbidden
To eat from the Tree of Life
Can we assume that the Gods
Intended them to eat from that tree,
So that they would live forever—
Without the knowledge of Good and Evil?)

In a dream I found myself
Standing at the barred gate
To the Garden of Eden,
And I could see from the ground
That many people had stood there before me,
And I could see from the bar
That made fast the gate
That many had laid hold of it
But could not lift it
And had to return to their burdens.
Then, aware of my Presence,
A hushed voice from within asked,
"Who stands without that would enter here?"
And I answered,
"One who has no knowledge of Good and Evil,"
And I heard from within a joyful noise,
And the gate swung open for me.

....

I find a creepy many-legged bug
Trapped in my deep sink.
And even though the sudden sight of it repulses me,
I feel for it and drape an old towel over the side
So it will have a means of getting out when it encounters it.
But here's the thing that troubles me:
If I see one of these scary looking bugs
Sprinting across the basement floor,
I do not hesitate to step on it.

In a final attempt
To find some reason to go on living,
A desperate young man
Sits down before an old sage
And tells him of his hopelessness
And of his readiness to die.
The old sage listens carefully
Then looks off into an emptiness
And back into time
Recalling his own hour of desperation.
Then he looks kindly into the eyes of the man
Sitting before him,
Extends his arms,
And asks him to take his hands.
When the man has done that
The old sage says,
"I too have stood at the door of that Dark House,
And had I entered there
I would not be here now to take your hands in mine.
Think on that.
And of the life
Of one not yet born
Who may someday come to you in his extremity
As you have come to me."

....

Did you ever consider reading a novel backwards
And try guessing what happens at the beginning?

When I hear the dove
Coo out its melancholy morning call
It seems to come to me from far away,
Yet at the same time
I can't dismiss the sense
I'm harkening to a sound—
That's oh so very near.

....

On an island paradise
An Angel of Civility
Alternately shares dominion
With a voracious beast.
However, so long as the Angel of Civility stays awake
The Island is a place of peace and tranquility,
And the murderous beast sleeps soundly
In the back of a dark cave.
But when the Angel of Civility nods off and falls asleep,
The murderous beast is roused from its lair
And devours the inhabitants of the Island,
The devouring ceasing
Only when the gluttonous beast has gorged himself
And returns to its lair to sleep again.
And it's this falling asleep of the satiated beast
That wakens the Angel of Civility,
And peace and tranquility
Return to the Island Paradise.

Wouldn't you just know—
That "God" would be an infallible "man"!!
And that this manlike "God"
Would send his son—
Not his daughter, but his perfect son—
As the messenger of good news to his creations,
And that this son
Would choose a following of twelve disciples—
All men!
Think about that.
And the Catholic Church
Thought that a patriarchal model was a good one to follow
And they did—with infallible Popes,
With their Cardinals and Bishops and Priests—all men!!
And Islam...with Allah and Muhammad
And the twelve infallible Imams—all males—
Is even worse.
And both these major Western religions
Wait the second coming—
Of an infallible holy "man"!!
That should tell you all you need to know
About these two prejudicial Fraternities.

....

The years had piled up
And life had not been kind to her,
And she decided
To return to her childhood home,
Perhaps to find there the little girl she had been—
When she was young
And carefree

And full of joyful innocence,
And life stretched out before her
Like a Ribbon of Dreams.
When she finally arrived,
The house was still there,
But the magic of the house was gone,
And she realized
That no magic could bring it back again.
As she turned to leave
The face of a little girl appeared at the window
And for a moment her heart leapt up—
But it wasn't her.
Nevertheless, she smiled and waved "Hello,"
Blew her a kiss,
Then as she walked away
Turned back and smiled again—
And waved "Goodbye."

....

When I read the imperative:
"Feed my sheep,"
I know for sure
I have a problem with Christian thought,
For when I come across these three words
Two of them piss me off—
The narcissistic paternalism of the possessive pronoun,
And the demeaning metaphor—
"Baa! Baa!"
What's that you say?
You find the metaphor demeaning too?

The little clown toy was fashioned out of tin
And brightened up with colored paints,
And once wound up would wag its head
And wobble all about in the most amusing way.
But here's the thing:
Though he is just a silly animated toy,
He is conscious of himself!!
And he embraces the "reality" of his "life"
And finds himself positively delightful!
But here's another thing,
Even harder to imagine:
One day it occurs to him
That maybe he's not really real after all!
"Maybe I'm actually just a silly animated toy," he thinks.
But straining his tin brain to the limit,
He decides that it would be quite impossible
For a silly animated toy
To have the thought that he is not really real,
And he dismisses the idea as quite preposterous
And wobbles off,
Wagging his head in the most amusing way.

....

The story told was told by knaves and fools.
It wasn't really lies they told
But still the things they said were not all true,
Or only partly true,
And there were things they didn't know
And therefore couldn't tell,
And those things would have told a different story,
A story that they didn't want to hear,

Which is too bad
For had they just allowed the time
For all the truth to come to light
They wouldn't have wrestled an innocent man
Out into the dark of night,
And,
With howls and jeers the last sound ringing in his ears,
Hanged him from a crooked branch of an old tree.

....

One child saw another
Trying to dislodge a boulder from the ground.
"What do you think you're doing?"
He asked,
Not believing his scrawny friend
Would be trying to do something so clearly impossible.
"Ten men couldn't move that rock!
You'd need a bulldozer at least."
His grappling friend looked back,
Let a little smile break out on his face,
Wiped his brow,
Spit on his hands,
And said,
"Oh yeah? Just watch this!"
He didn't get the massive rock out of the ground.
But he pushed out his anal canal so far
It broke through the back of his pants—
Which really impressed his friend.

Our "Gods" are nothing more
Than projections of ourselves—
Supernatural beings with a "person"-ality.
Try thinking about the nature of "God"
From the point of view
Of a highly intelligent and imaginative butterfly—
Or Bengal tiger!

....

While on a short excursion off the road
To see what kinds of flowers
Grow along stretch of old abandoned railroad tracks,
I see ahead of me what first appears
To be a heap of trash dumped there along the bank,
But soon make out
A crumpled derelict discarded there instead,
Slumped up against a broken tree
And gazing vacantly down the run of tracks.
He glances up at me as I approach,
And I can see at once how ruined inside he is.
He does not speak,
But drops his eyes
And goes on gazing down the rusty tracks again
As if he half expects
To see a little wisp of smoke
And hear a whistle blow.
I nod at him
And mutter a salute of sorts
To let him know he's something more
Than just a refuse pile
(Though sad to say he's little more than that)

And as I pass him by
It comes to me
That maybe he's not waiting for a train at all
But looking down those empty tracks
And back in time
At the black smoke of his own failed life
That clanged and rumbled by
And out of sight—
And left him here—
Backed up against a crippled tree.

....

You have to be out of your mind
To experience "God."
I don't mean you have to be crazy-
Just "out" of your mind.
And all those who think they know "God"—
Well, it's all in their head.

....

When she was young
She fell in love with a beautiful little girl
Who was so fresh and full of life
And so much adored by everyone,
But when she got older and grew up
She found that she was never able to get over—
That little girl she used to be.

After school one day
One of the tough guys,
No doubt in an effort to prove his toughness
To his little band of ruffians,
Started in on a quiet little boy.
The quiet boy
Tried to ignore him
And made every effort to move away,
But the bully followed after him
Taunting him unmercifully,
And poking and shoving him,
Until finally and unexpectedly,
The quiet boy just couldn't take it any more,
Turned on his tormentor
And began to batter him with a ferocity
That bordered on the sublime!
It happened so fast and furiously
That the defenseless bully
Was saved only when he cried out
And his friends managed to pry the quiet boy away.
When the tough guy finally got to his feet,
His nose was bleeding
And the rest of his face was bright red—
Partly because of the hailstorm of little fists...
Somewhere along his way home
A quiet little boy
Squares his shoulders,
Examines the redness of his knuckles,
Then looks over at a barking dog—
And barks back!

Only the dead know the meaning of life,
And if life has no meaning—
Even the dead don't know it.

And if life is ultimately absurd—
And if there are degrees of absurdity—
Then a person is absurd
In proportion to the meaning he finds in that absurdity.

However—
All is relative.
So isn't it quite possible—
Quite probable, in fact—
That life IS meaningful here an now
To a person who is now here,
But has no meaning to a person
When that person is no longer alive and here now?

And if this is truly the case,
Isn't it kind of tragic
And evidence of an abject vanity
When someone forfeits his chances
For meaning and happiness in this world
Because he believes,
In doing so,
He will receive it more abundantly
In the next?

It has been said that
"Love is a many splendored thing,"
And it truly is—
Until half of it dies.

....

If there were no sentient beings on planet earth
To be conscious of the Moon,
Would there still be a Moon?
And in the absence of an observer
Anywhere in the Cosmos,
Would there even be a Cosmos?
I have heard it argued that there would not be.
But if there were no Cosmos—
This seems uncomfortably obvious—
Sentient beings would never have evolved
To be conscious of it!
How we perceive it
And what we make of it
May be all in our heads
But our heads are here,
And it took some Cosmic doing to get them here.
And if what we call the Moon and the Stars
And the Cosmos at large
Don't exist in the absence of sentient observers,
Then I can only conclude
That not only the observed,
But the observers also,
Are figments of an imagination
Considerably more expansive
Than my own.

I was once confronted by a troublesome inquisitor
Who advanced the proposition
That a watermelon is not red inside
But only turns red
When exposed to light,
Which he explained happens instantaneously
When it's cut into,
And challenged me to prove otherwise,
Which I couldn't,
But to let him know how unseriously
I regarded his proposition
I advanced one of my own
Proposing that inside every watermelon
A wee leprechaun slumbers near the green rind,
And at the first break in the rind,
Wakes with a start,
Becomes invisible,
And charms unseen out of the melon
And into a distant emerald realm
Where it finds a stand of Shamrocks to shelter in—
And challenged him to prove me wrong,
Which he couldn't.

....

What is Life
But Death
Dreaming itself awake,
And what is Death
But Life waking from a Dream.

In a flat, two-dimensional "reality"
A creature able to imagine
A world of three dimensions
Would either be regarded as a visionary—
Or one that has "left the plane."
And I can't help but wonder
If Subtle Entities,
Existing in a multi-dimensional scape,
Would find our three-dimensional consciousness
Almost unimaginable.

....

The old man was gruff and abusive
And menaced children
Who stumbled into his yard,
Frightening them away
With flailing arms
And fiery imprecations.
They called him "the bogey man."
And when strangers,
Unaware of the ogre inside,
Knocked on his door
They fared no better.
But it is rumored
That on dark summer nights
If you stand in the shadows
And listen very carefully
You can hear the bogey man
Inside his blackened house
Sobbing his heart out.

One child picks up a rock
And throws it through a window;
Another picks up a rock
And appreciates the heft and beauty of it.
Why do they "choose" two different things?
When you are able to fully answer that question
You will have rolled a great stone
Over the grave of "free will,"
And the Cosmos will call you by your first name.

....

Master, is there life after death?
Go away. You are not worthy of my counsel.
But how have I offended you, Master?
Do not come back to me
Until you can answer that question for yourself.

....

If you know what you're looking for
You are likely to overlook
All the things not in your line of sight,
And it may be
That among the very things you overlook
Is the very thing you're looking for!
For that reason, I don't look for something—
I just Look
And don't allow what I'm looking for
To limit what I see.

The ink inside my well is all used up,
All scribbled out upon these many sheets
That clutter up my table top.
I guess I always knew this day would come,
When I'd run out of ink,
And so I sigh and lay my pen aside.
The hour's late
And I am tired to the bone
And should have turned in long ago.
A scraping sound as I push back my chair
And stand and stretch my arms and yawn.
I'm so done in I feel as though
I'm just about to fall in love with Sleep.
I shuffle to the door,
And stop to cut the power to the light
That hangs above my desk,
But then decide to leave it on—
I wonder why I'm doing that? I ask myself.
Maybe I have it in my head somewhere
That I'll be coming back,
But I can tell you now I won't.
Or maybe I just want
To leave behind a little Light—
That's it, I think:
I want to leave behind a little Light.
And that thought comforts me.

Well, old faithful resting place,
I'm here at last to turn your cover back
And lay me down.
I hope I'm not too tired to dream.

Do you believe in God?
Not in the God that you believe in.
But you believe in God of some kind?
I search for "God"
I long for "God"
I am in love with the idea of "God."
But no, I do not believe in a God of some kind.
Why wouldn't you imagine a God you could believe in?
I would not limit "God" with my belief.
How can you be content to not believe in God?
Harken well to what I say:
The Mystery of God moves through me
Like a current of Light
That brightens every atom of my being,
And my heart trembles
At the Beauty of my unbelief.
I am content to Wonder "God."

....

We humans are now
In the "gregarious" phase,
Multiplying and swarming,
And in our frenzy
Consuming the lush Biology of our Planet,
And nothing appears able to stop us
Until we have devoured
Our "Mother,"
And in the bargain—
Ourselves!!

Some mystics believe that
Being born is the first step in losing Consciousness,
And growing up
Is really a process of growing down,
Consciousness speaking;
And then some who have grown low down
Realize what has happened to them
And life becomes a spiritual quest
To regain Consciousness.

Now, mystics believe that can be accomplished here,
And that some have done it.
I know one such.
Unfortunately—
At least I find it unfortunate—
This one that I know
Believes that only those
Who have completed this "Great Work" here
Are in some sense "saved" in the hereafter,
Giving him something disagreeably in common
With the born-again Christians that I know.

I have wondered about that—
The selective salvation of certain souls—
And my mind has rejected the notion.
Then I think of Natural Selection:
In the biological world,
And the fact that only the most fit
Are "selected" to survive,
And the rest perish—in numbers!
And I wonder if that evolutionary fact

Isn't quite consistent with
The selective salvation of certain souls?
Despite that wondering,
I am still persuaded
That everything in the Cosmos
Cycles into and out of being what it is
And only Essence "remains"—
Neither Planets or Stars or Galaxies are excepted—
And neither are special men and women,
Whatever "great work" they "accomplished."

(There is also this:
I find no reason to believe
That the Essence of the Cosmos
Is obliged to be consistent
With the dynamics of biological evolution.)

....

When I saw him
I could see at once he was a "casualty,"
Not of some clash of arms
Or serious accident,
But a victim of some internal violence,
Quite severe, it appeared to me,
Probably from a deep wound to his heart.
Oh, he tried to hide it
But there was no hiding
The "blood" coming out of his eyes.

I am running down a corridor.
It's long and narrow and brightly lighted
And at the far end of it
I can make out a closed door
Which I can't take my eyes off,
For it seems my very life
Depends on getting to that door,
And yet with every step
My legs are getting so heavy
That I begin to despair that I will ever reach it,
But finally, somehow,
Nearing complete exhaustion,
I arrive at the door
Only to find that it's made of heavy steel
And welded into place!
And then there is this—
At first I think it is the blood
Throbbing in my ears,
Due to my exertions,
But to my horror I realize
That what I'm hearing
Is the muffled sound
Of someone pounding
On the other side of the sealed door!
And I wonder if you can imagine the alarm I feel
And the sheer panic I experience
When I have this certain knowing
That the person pounding on the other side—
Is me!

A raindrop falls upon the earth
And wets a spot
Then disappears
And is forgot
Like people's tears.
Had it been cold enough to snow
It would have wafted to and fro
And landed soft somewhere
Perhaps upon a rooftop near
Or in a little girl's hair.

....

I taught my two young daughters
That the little tan spiders
That lodged in the corners of our ceilings
And sometimes dangled
Magically in the air,
And now and then traipsed about on counter tops,
Were valued house guests
And should be made to feel welcome.
I also made it clear to them
That they were very fragile little creatures,
And even a gentle touch could injure them.
And in teaching them that
I was reminding myself
That my two young daughters
Were fragile little creatures too.

Land mine...
A carefree child
Bounces through a field of Yellow flowers
Chasing Butterflies,
Her hair dancing freely about her face,
The Sun a warm simile in the Sky.
Her heart is light
And she is laughing.
Life to her is a thing that flutters...
When she wakes from her coma
And finds both her shortened legs
Bandaged at the knees—
Yellow is no longer a color
And nothing flutters in the room.

....

The loss of memory is the loss of everything

....

A friend of mine sent me this quote
(Conrad, if I remember right):
"I have known two men, too much alike.
Neither took a breath but he did it for love and honesty.
One found himself making wine out of water.
The other found himself making water out of wine."
He clearly saw me as the latter man
And intended these words as a reproach,
But I took them as a compliment.
After all, Water is the "fountain" of Life,
And what is wine but a yeasty fermentation?

The odds of a planet evolving
Similar to planet Earth
And of life beginning on that planet
And evolving into a contemplative species,
Contemporary with our own,
Are very long indeed,
But the odds of another such planet
In our galactic neighborhood
Doing that during the same brief survival interval
(For a mammalian species
About a million years)
Are "astronomical"!!
And for either one
To conquer time and space to reach the other—
The odds are almost inconceivable!
Yet I still believe we are not alone—
Not here in our corner of the Milky Way—
And perhaps not here on this blue planet Earth!!

....

"Pull yourself up by your bootstraps"
Is good advice for those
Who are not impoverished inside,
That is,
For those who have inner "boots"
With "straps" on them—
And sinewed inner arms.

I'm watching a play in a dark theater house,
And the odd thing is—
I'm in it.
And odder still
I seem to be directing it—
But I'm not.

....

Imagine this:
You are suddenly transported
Into a "vault" of intergalactic space
Where it is profoundly dark and still,
And you feel as one entombed.
But at length your eyes discern
A tiny swirl of misty light
That somehow you know
Is your own Milky Way,
And looking at that wee curlicue
Out there in its remoteness
It occurs to you
That if you immediately set off for it,
Approaching at the speed of light,
That after a lifetime of travel
It would still look to you then
Just as it does now,
Still just a smudge
In the enormity of black—
But the good news is
You don't have to get there—
Just stop imagining that you are here!

Where are you going?
I don't know.
But you seem so intent on getting somewhere.
Oh, I am.
But you don't know where?
I told you I did not.
Does it bother you not to have a destination?
It would bother me if I had one.
Why is that?
Because then I would know where I'm going.
Then you actually enjoy not knowing where you're going?
I do indeed.
And why is that.
I want to be surprised when I get there?
Well, how will you know when you get there
If you don't know where you're going?
That's the beauty of it!!

....

It is possible
To be so preoccupied with your inner world
That you lose contact
With the world at large,
But it is also possible
To be so in touch
With everything external to you
That you lose contact with yourself.

Read the Parable of the Sower.
Think about it.
Do you see the outstretched arms
Of the understanding and compassionate Rabbi
As he speaks?
Knowing what you know about the heart of this man,
Can you hear the deep wisdom in his words?
But I caution you not to read
The verses that follow.
If you love the just and gentle Rabbi,
Do not read
The words that Mark puts
Into his mouth.
Especially do not open your ears
To his explanation
Of why Jesus teaches in parables.

....

The idea of animal sacrifice—
To appease the gods—
Is a profanity,
As if one could placate a wrathful god
By killing an innocent creation of "God."
And the idea
Of "God" offering up his own blood sacrifice
To appease "himself"
To me is an utter absurdity.
(It is an absurdity to me
Even to imagine a wrathful god.)

As an old woodsman sits at his table
Smoking his pipe,
A young beast emerges from the dark forest
And scratches at his door.
The old man feels for the desperate creature
And gives him a bowl of broth.
"Oh thank you so much,"
Says the youthful creature.
"You are so kind."
And he laps it up
And disappears back into the dark forest.
Some months later,
The beast—
Now considerably larger than before—
Returns again and asks for something to eat.
This time from his meager store
The kind man
Gives the growing beast a piece of meat.
When months later the beats returns,
His eyes are narrow and intense,
And he snarls at the man
To give him whatever food he has.
And when he has greedily scarfed it down,
The beast demands more,
And when the man tells him his pantry is bare,
He eats the man.

....

Think about this:
That we ARE the missing link!

The Spirit of Creation
Evolves and Abides
In all that IS—
In every Atom,
In every Star,
In every animated form.
And my heart and mind
Embrace it in its entirety
Without exception or exclusion.
I call this Intimate Connection
Oneness—
Which sometimes feels to me like Love.
It does not expect my thanks or gratitude,
Nor even my Acknowledgment,
Nor my Acceptance,
Nor my constant Appreciation.
But I feel these things for it.
It is not good or evil,
Nor cognizant of good and evil,
And therefore does not judge.
And those who fear it
Do not understand it.
To me—
It is simply something I Recognize—
Something I am.

....

The mystery of God is confounding even to God

I see a virtually worthless object
Displayed in a shop window—
The price absolutely preposterous!!
I go in and accost the shopkeeper:
"Excuse me, Sir,
But the object in your window,
Is outrageously overvalued."
"Is it now?" he muses,
As if he knows something which I do not.
Then he leads me to a full length mirror
And asks me to stand in front of it,
Which I do.

....

I am the bar-headed goose
Slow-rowing high above land,
Breathing thin air,
And I am the ghost crab
Breathing through gills,
Chambered in sand.

....

A woman sits at a little window
Situated in the eye of God,
Unmindful of her holy observation post,
Peering out,
Wondering if God is out there somewhere
Mindful of her.

Try to imagine the consciousness you had
Before you were born,
When you were still in your mother's womb,
Before you "personified."
Can you do that?
Can you clear your mind
Of all you now imagine that you are
And journey back
To that prenatal state of being
Where your conscious brain
Simply effervesced and tingled Possibility!
If you can do that
Then you have come as close to "making one"
With the All of Everything
As it is likely you will ever come.
But if that is not close enough—
And if you can—
Then regress the entire Cosmos
Back to the moment before its Genesis,
Back into that timeless and spaceless "Womb"
"Where" out of seeming nothing
All Possibility birthed itself into Being,
And everything that never was,
And never could have been,
In that bright birthing moment of creation,
Suddenly had a chance to be!
And after you have trembled
With the unborn and birthing Cosmos
Come back to this present time and place
And the person that you are,
And open every sense you have

And just let your consciousness experience
The Stupendous Marvel of it All!!!

....

After the "good thief"
Had chided the other for mocking Jesus
He asked Jesus to remember him
When he came into his kingdom,
And after Jesus reassured the good thief
That he would be with him in paradise that very day,
I like to think
He turned and looked at the other thief,
And that his heart opened to him,
And that he said to him,
"And you, my suffering brother,
Who has been more sorely wronged
Than I or this other,
You too will I see in paradise this very day."

As it turned out, of course,
That meeting had to be delayed—
According to scripture
As many as forty days!!
(Curious to me that Jesus
Was alive for well over a month
After he was removed from the cross!
And that there is not more
Written in the Gospel record
Or in the Acts of the Apostles
About what things he said and did
During those forty extraordinary days!)

The Cosmos is Beautiful to me
Not because it is steadfast,
But because it is not;
Not because it cares,
Because it doesn't;
Not because it will someday come
To judge the quick and the dead,
But because it won't;
It is Beautiful
Just because it IS!!

And the marvels of the wild kingdom
Are not Beautifully designed creatures
Because Nature is a compassionate and forgiving designer.
They are Beautiful and marvelous
And incredibly diverse
Because she is not—
It's replete with biological wonders
Only because "it's a jungle out there."

....

When I ponder the phenomenon
Of my own self consciousness
I get this sudden sense of dislocation or detachment—
Exponentially more stunning
Than an out-of-the-body experience,
More like an out-of-the-mind experience—
As if I were a "densely" programmed computer
That suddenly became conscious of itself!

An elderly woman slumps on a park bench,
Head looking down at her hands.
She is convulsing with sobs.
A cat sits at her feet,
Beautiful and Indifferent.
I sit down at her side,
Ask if there's something I can do.
She cannot speak.
After some moments,
Very slowly,
She turns toward me
And extends her folded hands.
I wrap them in my own.
But when I gently pressure them
She pulls back,
"Oh please be careful," she sobs.
I follow her eyes down to our hands.
Gradually she opens them to me
And I see what she has been holding
And understand her grief.
At that moment her cat turns
And looks up at us,
Beautiful and Indifferent.

....

She had achieved perfect humility
The only problem was
That in a secret place in her mind
She was proud of that.

Satan exists as a concept
Only because some of us are unwilling or unable
To see and accept the "darker" side of "God."
When we are able to see
That "good" and "evil"
Are simply moral impositions
That we place upon the Cosmos,
Then we will come to understand
That the concept of Satan
Is nothing more
Than a blindness in one eye
That keeps us from seeing
The Wholeness of "God,"

....

Many years have passed since...
Yet I have come back.
I approach on foot,
Stop on the corner across the street,
And remember—
The house itself,
The old woman inside,
(My beautiful Grandmother)
Her desperation,
The separate garage behind the house,
The rope tied to a rafter,
The toppled stepladder.

If I were the white-marbled David,
Standing in the Accademia Gallery,
And were gifted with a moment of self awareness,
I hope I would not look down at my large hands
And conclude that it was they
That held the mallet and the chisels that sculpted me.
And if I were Michelangelo,
Standing at the foot of "my" great work,
I think I'd look down at my large hands
As if they were not mine.

....

Not by faith,
Lest any man should boast.

....

To an old friend:
When you look at me
You see yourself as you once were,
And you see me
As I still am.
And if you cannot understand
How it can be
That I still am as I was,
It is just as true
That I cannot understand
How it can be—
That you are not now
As you once were.

Mid November night,
Alone in my easy chair,
Facing south,
Sun room to my left.
I turn to glance through it to an east window
And see a crescent moon resting
In her journey up the black sky,
A little south of due east.
What a pleasant sight to these old weary eyes!
(Though something slightly odd about it too, I think)
Some small time later I turn and look again.
"How can that be" I puzzle to myself
For it is lower now than it was before!
The moon through an east window
Is always on the rise!
I peer intently at the scallop image
And wonder hard...
It's then I note what struck me odd at first—
The curve is wrong!
And then I understand
The trick Reflection's played on me:
The "rising" crescent in the east
Is actually a crescent sinking in the west!

....

The thing that disturbs me
When an "unthinkable act" occurs—
Is that it then becomes "thinkable."
And having become thinkable
Becomes more likely to occur again.

When I think about my cat—
Closed up in my house as he is,
Deprived of the freedom to prowl about outdoors,
To hunt and fight and mate,
Always eating from a glass bowl
And wasting in a litter box,
I often wonder if he's troubled
By a vague feeling that something
Isn't quite right about his life,
And then I find myself
Caught in the act
Of self reflection.

....

He had never truly been tested,
And longed for a real challenge,
For "a dragon to slay"—
A dragon big enough
And fierce enough
To take his full measure.
And he got his wish,
But after the dust had settled
(And there was precious little of that)
It was the dragon
That stood the ground—
And then forlorned its way back to its lair
Longing for something
Big enough and fierce enough
To take its full measure.

Days before Christmas,
The morning overcast and gloomy,
A little old lady walking her small dog.
Sees where a string of blinking lights
Has fallen from a neighbor's shrub.
Goes up,
Struggles with them,
But finally gets them shambled up
And goes her way.
Just as she is tottering out of sight
The string of lights
Falls to the ground again!
My heart takes a little plunge.
Not wanting her
On her way home
To see her kindly work undone,
I venture out and get them hung just so.
Later,
Glancing from my window—
The old lady
Standing on the walk,
Inspecting her neat array,
Smiling,
A string of colored lights
Blinking in her grey eyes,

Some days after,
A note stuck to my front door.
"I saw what you did."

One day in the Land Without Risk
A tiny meteorite
Falls from the sky
And strikes a little boy on the head
Killing him instantly.
"We must see that such a thing
Never happens again,"
Says the King,
And he decrees that from that day forward
Everyone in the realm,
Must wear a special helmet,
And do you know that to this day
Not a single person in the Realm
Has been killed by a piece of falling sky!
The only problem is
Some people begin to die
From complications caused—
By wearing the special helmets!
So the King scratches his head
(He had exempted himself from wearing a helmet)
And declares,
"Now that the sky has stopped falling,
I am banning the wearing of helmets!"
And his subjects cheer their approval:
"Such a wise King we have," they cheer.

....

We became human
When we became ethical,
And we "fell from grace"
When we imagined a moral God.

"You made this, Papa?"
Said a young boy
Holding up an exquisite form
Sculpted out of wood.
Yes, I did—
But I had help.
"Who helped you, Papa?"
If you climb up here on my knee
I'll tell you,
Here let me help you up—
There you are.
Well, one day when I was a young man,
Many long years ago,
I stumbled over a block of wood
Lying on the floor of an old barn.
And I can't tell you why,
But something made me pick it up,
And as I held it in my hands and looked at it—
You promise you won't laugh?
"I promise I won't laugh, Papa."
I felt something yearning inside of it,
You know, longing to come out.
I'll never forget that strange sensation?
Anyway, I took it home with me.
And put it on the stand beside my bed.
And every night before I went to sleep
I'd take it in my hands and think about it.
Then one night,
I had a strange dream
And in it I saw—
Or thought I saw—

What it was inside that wanted out!
So the next day
I got out my carving knife and set to work.
Day after day I cut away at it,
But I struggled,
For though my knife was sharp,
The block of old wood was very hard
And seemed at odds with me,
Almost as if it didn't like what I was doing.
Well, I worked until my hands hurt
And places on my fingers bled.
Finally I could see the form emerging!
And from that moment on
It quickly started taking shape,
But just as I was nearly finished
My knife slipped!
In my haste to see it done
I sheered away a vital portion of the wood,
Making a ruin of the dream I had of the thing inside.
Oh, how could I have failed
So precious a piece of wood as this,
I grieved,
And failed the thing inside that yearned?
And how could I have so failed myself?
And then,
As I mourned the botched creation in my hands,
Suddenly my heart leapt up!
For in the damaged piece
I now imagined something else!
Something I never would have imagined
Had I not wrecked the dream I had,

Continued

And that something—
That special something—
Was the thing inside the wood that wanted out!
And that is what you're now holding in your hands.
"I really like that story, Papa."
Said the little boy
Looking at the polished piece of wood
His eyes wide—and Wondering.
"I think I know now what you meant
When you said you had a little help.
It was the knife that slipped, right?
But, Papa, the thing that yearned—
That wasn't really in the wood was it?
That was in you.

....

Eons from now
Some "alien" astronaut
Will emerge out of the interstellar wilderness
And gently maneuver his craft
Into silent orbit
Around a thriving planetary Biosphere.
I can imagine the wideness of his eyes
And the wonder in his mind,
As he looks out a viewing port
And sees for the first time
The quiet beauty
Of what—
Eons ago—
We called our Planet Earth.

Memories can be buried,
But they can't be killed,
And if they could be killed
The ghosts of them cannot.

. . . .

Some people can't see themselves as they are
So they dress themselves up inside as someone else
And go through life
Pretending that they are that other person,
And this often works so well
That some,
Even as they face death,
Are not able to face themselves.

. . . .

I can only feel a profound sense of pathos
For anyone who is moved to ask:
"Is this all there is?"
Such a person
Would find the Garden of Eden
A Wonderless wasteland,
And could visit heaven,
Sit down with God,
And within five minutes,
Would be looking at his watch.

During the 16th century
There hung in an abbey in Boxley, England
A large, "supernatural" image of the crucifixion of Jesus
Whose eyes and mouth could move,
And whose head could nod assent
If the holy image granted a supplication
Or accepted a penitence.
I wonder if it ever occurred to the monk—
Ensconced in a cabinet beneath,
Or an enclosure behind,
Manipulating the wires and levers—
That maybe there was something not quite right
About this unsupernatural manipulation
Of the holiest icon of Christendom,
Turning the crucified image of Jesus
Into a performing marionette!

....

A lone gunman
Breaks into an elementary school
With an automatic weapon
And ruthlessly murders twenty little children
And six staff members,
Then takes his own life.
The world mourns the 26 victims,
And my heart too goes out to them—
But I also grieve for the 27th victim.

A mound of moist clay on a Potter's wheel.
It doesn't feel the wet fingers
And gentle pressure
As the Potter pulls it up into a graceful vase.
Nor is it conscious
Of its greenware being trimmed and etched
Nor of the paints and glazes
And the many firings in the kiln.
Today it poses on a white tablecloth
In a fancy French restaurant
Where patrons often admire its style and charm,
Which makes it blush with pride—
For having made of itself
Something so Beautiful and True.

....

A woman,
Sits alone in a dark room.
Her soul desperately unsure.
She hears a voice utter her name:
"I have heard your wordless prayers,
And am moved by them.
Harken now to me."
But as she harkens,
The voice breaks off
And silence enters the room,
Shutting the door behind it.

There was something prehistoric in her eyes,
What some might call a "primal melancholy,"
An atavistic loneliness
Such as might have been seen
In the eyes of Eve
After she had been cursed
And driven from the Garden.

....

I dreamed a new and better Planet Earth
A world where the stain of man
Had been bleached out of the garment of life.

....

There are now more than 7 billion human beings
Disfiguring the Beautiful countenance of Planet Earth.
Is there a more hopeless observation than that?
But there is this optimism:
Were they all to perish this very moment
And fall to the ground and rot,
The odor of their decomposition
Would be gone in a matter of weeks,
And in a matter of geologic seconds
All traces that they were ever here
Would be forever erased
From the face of the earth.

In a just society
Everyone is "entitled" to an equal opportunity to prosper.
Given that, (which of course, cannot be given
Since we are all unequal in so many ways)
Inevitably those who have more initiative
And are more daring
And more creative
And more resourceful—
In short, who are more enterprising—
Will be more successful.
And they are "entitled" to prosper more.
The result is a kind of "social justice,"
Where rewards go disproportionally to the productive,
And members of the society
Accept unequal outcomes
As the cost of doing Freedom's business.
It is the lesson we learn from
And the homage we pay to
Natural Law.

....

It occurs to me that the only "unforgivable sin"
Is the notion that there is such a thing!
And even that "ungodly" sin—
Is forgivable.

....

To the extent that a person is conscious of his personal "self"
To that extent he is unconscious of "God."

Leafing through a scrapbook of her life,
She realized
That she was looking
At faces she didn't recognize
And places that were unfamiliar.
She seemed so unconnected to it all.
And it frightened her
And she began to wonder
If she had ever really existed at all,
And she decided that she had not.

....

Every day for almost six years
People have gathered to watch a man
Approach a massive oak tree,
Squat before it,
Wrap his arms around the trunk of it,
And with every muscle of his body straining
Struggle to wrest the behemoth from the ground.
Finally one day
The man stood up after his failed effort,
Let out a heavy sigh,
And announced to the crowd
That he would not be back to try again.
"I cannot do it," he despaired.
It was painful for him
As he walked away
To hear the watchers jeer at him,
"Quitter! Failure! Poltroon!
You are not worthy of the task!"

After Cosmic Genesis,
The Cosmos expanded in Darkness
The duration of which was long and wonderless
("Long" having no meaning at that "time"
Nor any "time" since that "time" for that matter,
"Time" being quite imaginary as it is,
And "wonderless" only in the sense
That there were none to wonder it.)
Perhaps five hundred million years would pass!
And then!
Out of the expanding Darkness,
In the gathering clouds of hydrogen and helium particles—
As if by magic,
The first Stars ignited!!
And Light was born!
That is, the physics of Light,
For the Cosmos would be blind
For several billion "years."
Strange to wonder that—
A Cosmos unable to see the Light of Itself.
And strange to wonder this:
What led up to the Genesis of our Cosmos?
What was on the other side of Creation.
Was it the mother of all black holes
That had gathered up
The remains of other expired Cosmic Systems
And rebirthed them?
Or was it the Eye and Mind of the Cosmos
Beginning,
For the first and only time,
The long process of Opening!

A man,
Standing on a dark stage
Facing a large white screen
Watching the flickering projection of his life,
His black shadow
Casting an image on the screen.
When the film runs out
The screen becomes grainy white,
Except for the dark figure on it,
And as the man contemplates his shadowy remains
He listens hypnotically
To the slap-slap of the take-up reel
Slowly spinning itself to rest behind him.

....

God is a walled Garden
Which you can only enter
By staying outside.

....

Take two:
"God" is a walled Garden
Which you can enter
Only by placing the palms of your hands
Upon the stones
And realizing that what you're feeling
Is the Inside of the Wall!

Two kittens of the litter left,
Struggling to survive,
One, healthy and strong and beautiful,
One small and sickly,
Unlikely to survive the night.
I have to choose between them—
To save only one.
I want to take the thriving one,
But my heart goes out to the struggling runt,
And so I do what Nature wouldn't do:
I choose the small and sickly one.

....

True Love is when you love something
That can't love you back.

....

Looking down
Scratching the head of Ol' Scruff,
A friend of mine
Is moved to comment:
"God should have stopped
After he made the dog."
I consider reminding him
That it was man who "made" the dog,
But I am caught in a reflection of my own:
"God should have stopped
After he made the wolf."

The Cosmos:
Quintessentially random,
Rational in every exhibition,
Unintentional,
Compulsively Evolutionary,
Uncompromisingly Utilitarian,
Dynamically interconnected,
Every ongoing expression of it Inevitable.
Not conscious
Nor caring
Nor moral
Nor judgmental
Confoundingly Existential!

....

The Cosmos is like a book
That has already been written—
And our lives but little stories
That have already been told.
Religious folk call it predestination;
I call it Inevitability.

....

I know we are not alone in the Cosmos
Because the law of probabilities forbids it.
If you jumped into the Cosmic haystack
You would come out a cushion of needles.

"Does a man have free will?"
No.
"Then he is not morally responsible for his actions?"
He is not.
"Then what would keep him from doing whatever he wants?
Since he doesn't have to fear the judgment of God?"
You forget there is another little matter—
He has to fear the judgment of man.

....

The Atom is God's surest witness
And how compelling
That a typical cell in my body has a hundred trillion Atoms
And that my body has over a hundred trillion cells!!

....

"God" is a great Sphere
And what is most strange about it—
Exceeding the wonder of even the most wise—
Is that the outside arc of it
Curves in upon itself!

....

Nowadays people like to say,
"It's all good."
And I guess it is,
But only if the concept of "all"
Is large enough
To include
Everything that's "bad."

I live next door to a little girl named Lucia.
She's about nine years old—
And blind.
Her mother has told me
That as an infant
She had some sensation of light,
But by the end of her first year
Even that was lost to her,
She's a bright girl
Who moves about in a dark world.

It's the day before Christmas,
Mid afternoon.
I see the family from my window,
Busily making preparations
To set out luminaries again.
Something they have done for several years now.
They work as a team,
Dad helping Lucia empty a scoop of sand into a paper sack,
The younger brother putting in a votive candle,
And Mother setting the bags in the wagon.
When the wagon's full
They set off,
Mother, Dad and younger brother,
Placing four bags
In front of each house,
Evenly spaced,
Near the curb,
Lucia pulling the supply wagon,
Her guide pole
Making sure her way.
Then it's back for another load.

It takes them nearly two hours
To take care of all the houses on our street,
But finally they finish.
I watch as they pass my house,
Returning home,
The younger brother running ahead
To catch up with Dad,
Lucia, holding her mother's hand
And pulling the empty wagon behind her.

Later, as darkness is about to fall
On the sighted world,
I decide to go out for an evening walk,
And as I move up the street,
I see Mother and Dad
Ahead of me,
Squatting in the cold,
Lighting the candles in the lantern sacks,
Lucia and her younger brother
Tagging along
"Watching" and chattering from the sidewalk,
Two happy little elves.
As I pass them
I am moved to say to the father,
"What you do is an act of neighborhood love,"
And he takes a step closer to me
And levels me with this hushed confession:
"Actually, we do it for Lucia."

It's then I realize that Lucia
Doesn't move around in a dark world after all.

I am a great ape
Born in captivity.
Do you wonder my bewilderment?
My profound loneliness?
The desperation I feel
Knowing that there's something so vital
My brain no longer remembers—
And something so natural and true
My heart can never forget?

And I am man,
But like the great ape
I am haunted
By the ghosts of my ancestral past,
And worse than that—
Or perhaps more Wonderful than that—
I am haunted by
Whisperings from the night sky,
The remote
But always present
Promptings from Beyond—
The call of the Sublime!

Sometimes they leave me,
And I am nothing but a loneliness,
But at times during every day
And always at night when I lay me down
The soft reverberations of them
Comfort me
And gentle me to sleep.

When you become unconscious of your "self"
(Of even the smallest detail of your personal life programming)
And yet retain a state of consciousness—
When you are conscious of nothing
But consciousness itself—
Then you know what it's like
To BE—
And "not to be"?
What it means to Make One!

....

The life of each of us is a portrait—
But not a self portrait.

....

The jagged knife of Guilt
Has rent and lodged itself into a woman's heart,
And the agony of it
Is more than she can bear.
And in her desperation,
She falls to her knees and cries out to God:
"My sins are so many
And so vile I can not speak them.
Can you ever forgive me?"
And after some while looking off into the void
God says to the woman:
"The knife in your heart.
Is a self-inflicted wound:
You must forgive yourself."

A Cow is grazing peacefully in a field
When a mouse rears up on its hind legs,
Reaches up from the grass
And pokes it in the face.
"Why did you do that?"
Asks the cow,
Quite surprised to be gobsmacked like that.
"I have done nothing but chomp grass
And Dream of greener pastures."
"Because while you were dreaming of greener pastures
You stepped on my brother
And mashed him!" screams the mouse.
The cow looks down at his foot,
And then back at the mouse.
And his heart caves in upon itself:
"I'm so sorry, little mouse.
I meant no harm.
Can you ever forgive me?"
And a tear falls from his eye
And splashes onto the head of the mouse,
Whose own little heart
Then caves in upon itself.

. . . .

Most adjust well enough
In a world of make believe,
But what of those few
Who must find their peace in a world
Where Truth is not escapable?

A little girl sits on a bench in her back yard,
Enchanted by the warbles of a tiny bird,
Ensconced somewhere in the leafy wilderness
Of a nearby tree.
She peers intently into it,
Hoping to see the tiny Wonder,
When of a sudden
A Bright little Creature flits to small branch,
Pauses there a long moment,
Then vaults from the branch
And lands on the little girls' knee,
Where it tilts its head
Looks up at her,
And begins to sing.
When the child tries to pet his back
With a finger,
The little bird flies away.

....

It is the Scientists of this world
Who are slowly and methodically telling
The Greatest Story Ever Told.
And it comforts me to know
That if there are other inquisitive beings
"Out there,"
As surely there must be,
They are likewise,
Slowly and methodically,
Telling the same story!!

When I was young
And thought there might be something like God,
I beat the bushes of my mind with a fury
Until I had knocked off all the leaves
And left the bushes standing there
A stark array of beaten stems
And broken twigs,
And in the bargain
Worn myself out.
But out of my futility,
Something like God came to me.
It was not God,
But something more abiding,
More wonderful than God.

....

I looked everywhere for God,
An found God everywhere I looked—
In the silent plenitude of glinting stars
And under every rock.
And never found a thing
That shouldn't be
Just as it is.
("Evil" is just the word we give
To works of "God"
We don't consider "Good")
So perfectly composed,
The Cosmic face:
Not one Immortal Atom
Out of place!

"God" is the Hidden,
Mysterious and Inaccessible,
Yet the explosive emergence of the Cosmos,
And every evolutionary change in it since then,
Is all Revelation!!
"God" is the Manifest,
Overwhelming every sense!!

....

The man heaped high praise on his old friend:
"He came out of nowhere
To dominate his field.
He dreamed big,
And wrestled his dreams awake!
A phenomenon, that's what he was,
Elemental and visionary.
The world will wait long
To see another of his like."
When he had spoken thus,
I wondered what had become of such a man.
"Is he still alive?" I asked.
When he looked at me
A sadness came into his eyes:
"Yes, I suppose you can say he is still alive.
You can find him today
Mumbling to himself
In the dreary lobby
Of the old Northern Hotel."

A clear plastic bag,
Half filled with cloudy water,
Tied at the top.
A small tropical fish,
Confined, trapped,
Darting frantically to and fro.
A hand lifts the bag,
Carries it to an aquarium
And spills the little fish into the water.
"Oh, thank you, God,"
It bubbles out;
"You have set me free!"

. . . .

In all the wild kingdom
Only one creature
Is able to contemplate his own death,
And because that creature has decided
He's too important to die—
He has "divined" a plan
To secure his immortality,
And that plan is based on the assumption
That a supreme, manlike "God" exists,
And that that "God" loves and values man
As much as man loves and values himself.
(Man is not the apple
Of "God's" eye;
Man is the apple
Of his own eye.)

A little girl looks into a mirror.
It looks like her,
But she knows it isn't really.
"Only an impostor," she says,
And she goes away.
When she comes back
She looks into the mirror again
And sees the same reflection.
"I was wrong," she thinks.
"It's really me."

....

Why does "God" have to be a man?
Why a heavenly father?
(I think we all know why)
Why not a heavenly mother?
Why either one?
Why not a concept without gender—
Or paternal/maternal nature.
I kind of like what "god" "said" to Moses:
"Ehyeh-asher-ehyeh,"
"I am that I am"
God is the "Am-ness"!!
Be-ing Itself!!
To say of YHVH more than this
Is to say too much.

Truth is a bird of prey:
Its wings are feathered,
And it flies where the air is thin.
But its eyes are keen,
Its talons sharp
And its beak
Designed to rip and tear.
It is Beautiful in the High Sky,
But when it dives,
It asks no quarter—
And it gives none.

So woe to all the phony things
That try the open ground—
The grand deception and the little lie—
When Truth, without a sound,
Folds back its wings
And plummets from the sky.
And woe to the unwitting prey
Who trusted that their "truth"
Was True,
And felt its talons strike—
And run them through.

....

The Cosmos is a mirror
Which "god" holds up
To see what "he" looks like.

I sometimes fancy
The Cosmos
"Intentionally" evolved us
Not to serve or fear or worship IT
But so that IT
Could Sense itself
And Wonder itself
And Reason itself,
Perhaps at last
To Recognize—Itself!!

....

She was so sensitive,
Not only to all things in this world,
But to things not of this world.
She told me once
That when she's standing
Out on a clear night,
Alone in the Stillness,
Looking up,
That she can feel
The warmth of the Stars
On her Face.

....

Though the Cosmos is manifestly liberal—
In essence and action
It is perfectly conservative.

Sometimes when designing something
The initial result
Is clumsy, makeshift, rudimentary,
Perhaps not functional at all,
And changes are made,
Modifications,
Improvements,
And maybe it's a little better.
The alterations and adjustments continue,
More experimental trials and errors,
Until finally a working model "Emerges,"
But even after that
Additional refinements are necessary,
Especially as performance requirements change.
The design process is always a work in progress,
The "finished" product always "Evolving."

Would those who scoff
At the concept of "Intelligent Design"
Also scoff at the proposition
That the Cosmos
Is unfolding in strict adherence
To rational principles?
Evolutionary process,
Whether material or biological,
Is logical and methodical.
It's not far-sighted,
Can't see beyond its nose, in fact,
Is maybe even blind,
But it feels its way along
As if it knows where it's going

And it seems to be getting somewhere.
It's certainly not wandering about
Like an idiot chasing an imaginary friend.

....

In a capitalist economy,
Where individual freedom is prized,
And inequalities are accepted,
It is those who are responsible and self reliant and hardwork-
ing—
(Yes, and to some extent the fortunate)
In short, who are enterprising—
Who are most valued and rewarded,
And it is the dull and inept and the lackadaisical—
(Yes, and to some great extent, the unfortunate)
Who are most disadvantaged;
And in a collectivist economy
Where inequalities are not accepted,
And "Social Justice" is imposed
It's just the other way around.
I never saw a colony or a hive or a herd
Or any other bio-collective
That inspired me as a model
For human society.

....

Tell me the date of a man's birth
And the exact place where he was born
And I will write his biography.

Compassion has been my undoing.
What keeps "God" strange to me
Is my inability
To be Indifferent to suffering innocents.
Yesterday I watched
A "fledgling" rabbit,
A gentle little herbivore,
Nibbling the clover in my backyard.
This morning I found its furry remains
Stuck to the damp grass
Fluttering in a light breeze,
And somewhere I knew
A nocturnal predator
Was dozing languidly
Digesting an easy meal of flesh and blood.
I can accept with philosophical equanimity,
The death of the small creature,
But not the short bout
Of frenzied terror
It experienced
Or its squeals of pain and desperation
As it fought for its life
With every fiber of its being.
But "God" is not moved by such things
As I am moved.
And I cannot be like "God,"
And that is my failing,
My undoing:
Why "God's" remains so strange to me—
Because I Feel,
Because I Care.

I'm afraid it's just not true,
What we were told
About the "single sparrow" falling,
And it is clear to me
That the gentle little herbivores of this world
Will not inherit the Earth.

(Oh, I know I romanticize
The "gentle little herbivores"
Who if left to their reproductive devices
Would breed out of control
And cause an ecological disaster
In the wild kingdom,
Likely ending in its own mass perishing.
I understand that.
And I accept the genius of "mother nature"
And the Cosmos at large.
I may even understand and accept
The necessity for pain and suffering
In the evolutionary process.
But it wrecks me emotionally.
And I am wondering
What evolutionary advantage
Such emotional sensitivity and empathy can have,
And I'm thinking—
It doesn't have any,
May in fact confer on the likes of me
A survival liability.)

Man was not condemned
And cast out of the Garden
For disobeying "God."
Man is the complicated and conflicted creature he is today
Because he evolved in a jungle,
Learned the "law of jungle,"
And is still burdened
By the raw brutality of that jungle law.
He was not accursed of God
For the sin of disobedience.
If he is "accursed" at all
It is because
He "obediently" evolved—
To be just as he Is.

And would we really want to change him
To purge him of his jungle wildness?
We have proved with the dog
That we can breed the wild out of the Wolf,
But do we really want to breed the wild out of the man?
To create a canine-like species of men
Who need to be fed and watered
By governmental handlers?
Would we really want
To become the grateful and loyal "companions"
Of a caretaker State?
To "wag our tails" at the sight of our "masters,"
To lick their hands?
To think that we,
Once proud and fiercely independent men,
Could breed ourselves

To such a grim submissive state as that
Where we serve the Great Leader
With cheerful willingness
And fawning gratitude!!

....

The "Kingdom" of my "God" is within me.
It maketh me a path to walk
And is a lamp unto my feet.
It is my Green field
And my Still Water,
And my shelter from the storm.
It is my Reason for being,
My Beauty and my Truth—
And though it loves me not,
It is my Beloved.

....

The dog had been beaten
And neglected
And finally abandoned in the back alleys
Where it turned into a mean and filthy cur.
When this wretched creature died
"God" took one look at it,
And wept.
He did not forgive the dog its many "sins."
He simply loved it.

The predatory beast
Of "man's inhumanity to man"
Is always hungry
And ever on the hunt,
And its victims
Are not only those it preys upon—
That endless host of suffering innocents.
It also devours the Compassionate Hearts
That witness its predations
And cannot close their eyes or look away.
Woe to those commiserating souls
Who take upon themselves
The individual hurts of all mankind.
For them
Every day is a kind of crucifixion.

....

While yet an adolescent malcontent
With old Khayyam I made the hours pass;
In taverns dimly lit I sat with him
And drank the Wine he spilled into my glass.

So many cups of Khayyam's wine I drank
I needed help to find the Tavern door,
But once outside the fresh air sobered me
Enough to know I wanted to know more.

I staggered to my room those nights alone,
And when next morn I'd wake and sit my bed
I'd find my tunic hanging on the post
All wrinkled up and stained a ruby red.

So much of what I drank from Khayyam's Cup
Unsettled me and jarred me from my seat,
But then, and now, I must confess I found
The bitter Wine he poured was bitter Sweet.

Some think Khayyam a perverse renegade
Who conjured up his heresies to lead
The disenchanted minds of youth into
A blackened alleyway—without a Creed.

But if you study close the "blackguard's" words,
You'll find revealed there a Khayyam Code,
And though the Cloth would scorn it as a Way,
To pilgrim feet it serves an Open Road!

Of all the "holy" men I tried for Truth
Not one held out to me a lamp that shed
Authentic Light. I could have followed one
Of several "Sons"—but picked Khayyam instead.

....

The Front window of my house
Lets in so much Light
It lifts my soul right out of me,
And the Back window
Looks out upon a Darkness so complete
I have to turn away
To keep from being crushed by it.

I first heard the call of the bounding main
When I played on the docks as a boy,
And I took to the sea with a head full of dreams
And a heart full of courage and joy.

I have charted my ship by the Brightest Stars,
And battled the surge and the squall,
But I have planted my feet on solid planks
And am good for the long hard haul.

I have always been found where the wheel is,
My eye always trimmed to the sea;
And I've sung when the day was a peaceful glide,
And been fierce when I had to be.

I have steered where the waters are dark and deep,
And have always stood steadfast and strong,
For I know that a heart that is brave and true
Can never go very wrong.

At the top of my mast flies the flag that I made
From the cloth of my sailor heart;
It's been tugged at and torn by the teeth of the wind
But has never been torn apart.

And it's often I've stood on the deck at night
With a clutter of stars in my eye
And have run up a sheet in my heart to catch
Any breeze that might come from the sky.

I may not arrive at the bourne I seek,
May get lost in the storms of the day,
But I'm tied to my helm and will stay with my ship
Though Poseidon himself bar the way.

And if I go down to a watery grave,
Overwhelmed by a monster swell,
I will go with a heart that is fearless and glad
With my Ship that I loved so well.

....

It is written that Jesus wept;
It is not written that Jesus laughed.
I wonder if he did.
It's hard to imagine a Jesus who didn't laugh,
But harder for me to imagine
A Jesus who did.
The inhumanity of man,
To man and beast alike,
And to the biosphere itself,
Is no laughing matter.

....

Alone,
Late into night,
Looking up into the sky,
Basking in the quiet shed of stellar light,
My cup overflows
And spills all over me.

For "God" so loved the world
That he accepted responsibility
For the failings of his creations,
Opened his great heart to them,
And embraced them all,
Just as they are,
Even the most abused and ruined,
Especially the most abused and ruined.

....

Don Quixote
Valiantly quested in his own special "realm"—
He was comically delusional
But his delusional ideals were gloriously Chivalric,
And he spoke for them,
And fought for them.
And was heroic
Because he was always True to them,
And he was like a Beautiful Dream come true—
Until the end of his life,
When he regained his sanity,
Saw the foolishness of his ways,
And died denouncing his chivalric ideals,
Even to the point
Of including a provision in his will saying
That his niece would be disinherited
If she married a man
Who read books on Chivalry!!

Suppose the absence of "God"…
What is left?
Only the Enchanting Cosmos Itself!
The profusion of the Galaxies!
Our Sun!
The Earth!
The Stars in the night sky?
The amazing Biosphere!
The stunning Beauty and Violence of the Wild Kingdom!
The ferocious struggle of Life!
"Higher" consciousness—
And the part each one of us plays
As we Reason and Wonder our way
Through the exquisite and confounding
Mystery of it all!
GOD is simply the Presence of Everything—absent "god."

. . . .

"God" is reading a Book.
On one page of it,
On a single line of that page,
In a single word of that line,
In a single letter of that word,
Inside one of the black pixels
Of that letter—
The Book of our Life
Opens and closes,
Even as "God's" eye
Passes over it.

She loves to paint
And her brushes are always busy.
Some of her creations please her,
And she hangs them in he personal gallery.
Those that don't
She discards or paints over.
She does not hold her paintings responsible for themselves.
She does not say to one:
"Oh, you have made yourself so beautiful and good and true,
I will keep you always close to me,"
Or to another,
"Oh, you have made such a ruin of yourself
And are so beyond redemption
I will throw you in the trash and burn you to ashes."
She does not pass moral judgment on them—
Only her own artistic judgment.
If there is an Artist God
Who "saves" some of its creations and not others,
I imagine that Creator God like this.

....

God is not a legislator
Or a prosecutor
Or a judge
Or a heavenly father.
If God must have a predicate
Let it be this:
God is the need we have for God,
The Ghosting Presence
That haunts our "upper rooms."

"God,"
I am your accomplishment.
If you judge me,
I hope you are not too hard on yourself.

....

A canvas painting,
Standing on an Easel
Inside the Studio of God,
Becomes "morally" conscious of itself,
And believes
That some of its colors are "wrong,"
And some of its brush strokes
Not quite "right,"
And here a smudge
And there a bit of a smear.
"I have made such a mess of myself,"
Thinks the painting,
"I should be hidden in a closet
Or put out with the trash."
It does not occur to her—
That she is not the Artist!
And that her "flaws"
Are all part of The Perfection.

....

Something about Water Evaporating
Makes me happy,
Gives me hope.

Strange how some of us
In our declining years
Recall with pride
The many battles we have fought and won,
The many good and kindly ways
That we have changed the world,
While others,
Who have fought as hard and won as much
And changed the world in just as many kindly ways,
Remember only where we failed ourselves
And rue those failings.

....

Our trouble is not that we can't see the Truth,
Which is conspicuous to every Open Eye,
But that we can't accept it,
And so we make up mythologies
That are just plain silly,
But somehow—
So great is our need to believe them,
We believe them.

....

We have in common
With nearly every other creature
That struggles to survive
In the competitive biosphere
Of planet earth,
One necessary but terrible emotion—
Fear.

We cannot see "God" as "God" IS
Because we cannot see ourselves as we Are.
(Or is it the other way around:
We cannot see ourselves as we Are
Because we cannot see "God" as "God" IS.)

. . . .

How is it that Satan,
After being cast out of Heaven,
Some many human generations later
Reappears there with his angel followers
And gets an audience with God?
And not only gets an audience
But persuades God to allow him to test,
With terrible afflictions,
The faithfulness of righteous Job?
Did Satan and his entourage
Have visitation rights in Paradise??
And still have the status
To beard God in his den!

. . . .

The Cosmos spied me
And was curious,
And wondered me,
And at length leaned own
And took me up in its hand
And looked me over pretty good,
Then smiled
And put me in its pocket.

Can the Ego become an objective Observer
Of its own subjectivity?
Without some subjective frame of reference,
How can the word "observation" have any meaning?
I think it's possible for an ego
To observe itself "from a distance"
In a detached or non-judgmental way,
But after this remote viewing of itself
The observer must return to its subjectivity
If it wants to participate in its "reality."

....

One of the most spiritually disturbing
Concepts for me to contemplate is the Christian contention
That man was made
In the image of "God"—
Disturbing,
Not because of what it says about man,
Which would seem the highest flattery,
But because of what it says—
About "God."

....

All warm-blooded critters
Are innocent and adorable
When they are very young
And wobbly on their feet—
Kittens, puppies, lambs and such...
Even human toddlers
Are not without a certain appeal.

There is a door in your Room
Which has always been locked
And therefore never been opened.
One day a Mysterious Visitor
Offers you the key
And tells you
That on the other side of the door
Waits something Sublime and Wonderful—
Or something Horrible and Terrifying!
There is no way to tell which.
You are secure and happy in your Room
Just as it is.
Do you take the key?
Do you open the door?

....

The manifest Cosmos makes perfect sense—
Is immaculately consequential—
Until you reduce it
To its Infinitesimals,
But since the Infinitesimals
Are indifferent to Substantialities,
The manifest Cosmos still makes perfect sense.
And the infinitesimals?
Well, they're the ultimate Wonder!
The Unknowable Mystery
At the root of all Knowable things.

I think it true—
What Einstein has said:
That "God" is not malicious,
And I think Einstein would agree:
Neither is "God" benevolent.
The Cosmos evolves without Intent,
And if it had a Scales of Justice,
It would have but one obsession:
To stay in balance.

....

When the door of my "Temple" swings open,
My face turns up to the sky,
And the sound of a choir of Atoms
Brings Tears to my eye.

They well up there in the corners,
Exquisite and charged with awe,
But they leave a trail of sadness
As they fall.

....

Of all the specks of punctuation
Only one is a blasphemy—the period,
And only one is holy—
The Question mark!

....

People in a crowd
Have one thing in common: They're all alone.

What kind of a Father—
For a single act of disobedience—
Would curse his children
And drive them from his home—forever?
And if that Father later decided
He had been too severe in his judgment,
Would he not go in search of his children,
And when he found them
Tell them that he had forgiven them
And plead with them to come home with him—
Especially if the children
Were sorry for what they had done?
Wouldn't a loving Father do that?
Surely he would not take
The beloved family dog,
Completely innocent of any fault,
Punish that dog unmercifully,
Then have it killed
As a surrogate for the judgment
He had pronounced upon his offending children,
And then ask the children
To accept the sacrifice of the dog
As an act of reconciliation.
Surely he would not do that.
And what would it say of the children
If they accepted such an offering
And wept in gratitude—
That their father "so loved them."

Not on the hands of Judas,
Not on the hands of the Jews,
Not even on the hands of the Romans—
The blood of Jesus
Is on the hands of "God."

(The whole idea of a blood sacrifice—
Especially a human blood sacrifice—
To appease the gods
Or to win favor from the gods
Or as a show of gratitude to the gods
Is ignorant and barbaric.
And it's downright contemptible to think
That "God" should pick up such a hideous idea
And divine it into a plan of redemption!)

....

He looks at a poor soul
Skulking in the shadows
And then at me and whispers,
"There but for the grace of "God" go I,"
And the poor soul
Skulking in the shadows
Steals a look at us
And grumbles to himself,
"There go I
But for the rationed grace of God."

Striding hopefully down the road of his life,
Whistling a song of possibility,
A man stumbles over a rock,
Crashes to the ground,
And is knocked unconscious.
Some considerable time later
He comes to his senses
And finds himself sitting in the dirt,
A great throbbing in his head.
"Oh, now I will be late,
And my great opportunity will be lost," he sighs,
Not realizing
That being late to this appointment
Will make him right on time
For an opportunity
He could not have dreamed of!!

....

I am "found" in the galactic wonderland,
In the sparkling clutter of the night Sky,
In the natural environment of planet Earth.
I am even "found" in the hearts of beating Atoms;
But here,
Among the "cultured" ways of man,
In the midst of those
Who know what should and shouldn't be,
I am "lost."

Walking alone,
Turning over the soil of my mind,
Sorting through the loam of it,
But still alert
To all the stimulation of the day—
When of a sudden,
Close by and distinct,
The call of a Bird,
The sound of it
Enough to stop me in my tracks.
A long life
Attending to the songs of Birds,
And now this—
Somewhere up there,
Cloaked in that leafy wilderness,
Pouring out its feathered soul,
A new Voice!!
Are there new birds then—
Or has my "hearing" just improved?

....

Eyes are spiritual
To the extent that they
Are able to experience Beauty—
And the ablest of eyes
See Beauty
Everywhere they look.
(Even though She
Often wears a "hideous" disguise.)

When a mother,
Hoping to stir her daughter's imagination,
Asked her:
"If you were something that floats,
What would you be?"
The little girl
Thought for awhile
Then suddenly exclaimed,
"I know!
I'd be a bottle with a cork in it—
With a note inside!"
This answer surprised her mother.
"Why that's wonderful," she said,
"And the note? What would it say?"
And the little girl jumped to her feet,
And cried out gleefully:
"Oh, won't it be exciting to find out!"

....

Like the elephant,
Feeling the tremors in his feet,
I sense calamity
And want to head for higher ground
And take with me
All the blameless creatures of this world,
Find some safe place to hide
And wait it out,
Until the horror ends.
But there is no higher ground;
There is no place to hide.

"I want to show you something
That helps to keep me on my feet," he said,
And asked if I would follow him along a towpath
Leading round the barn,
Which I was glad to do.
He was old and wizened and walked bent over,
Steadied by a crooked stick.
(The two of them a perfect match, I thought.)
His voice was weak and haggard, like his legs,
And seemed to stagger through the air to reach my ears.
"Well, here we are," he said,
And raised his cane and gestured to the single tree
That barely stood its ground back there.
"Would you just look at that!" he beamed.
We planted twelve of them, my dad and I,
Our own small orchard right there behind the barn."
A smile warmed his face as he remembered that.
"This last of them that you see here
Should not be here,
Should be with those eleven other trees,
But there it stands, unlikely as that is,
And here I stand—sustained by it."
The frightful sight of that misshapen thing
At first took me aback—
So old and broken down it was,
The gnarled trunk of it half eaten by decay.
The only sign that it was still alive
A single bough of slender leafy stems.
And then it came to me,
Just what it was about the tree
That kept the old man "on his feet."

"It perseveres," I said. "And that inspires you.
It helps you stand your ground."
The old man looked at me
And something puckish passed across his face—
Then said:
"That's half the truth of it.
It does inspire me to rise each day
And put some weight on these two wobbly legs,
But in another way it also serves me well"—
And here he lifted up for me to see—
His crooked walking stick.

....

What does "God" see when he looks in a mirror—
The face of the Cosmos,
Which does not smile—
Or frown.

....

Halloween night.
Escaped from the house,
A black cat.
Black,
The color of grief
In a little girl's heart.
Yellow,
The color of her hope
That "Kitty" will be found.

"Come, Rabbi.
The hour is late,
We must make haste."
But even as I spoke
The Master lifted up his hand to quiet me
For he had heard a sound that troubled him
Coming from the shadows off the road
And turned his eyes that way.
Then with an urgency
He hastened to the well,
Filled up his cup,
And walked it down into a patch of dark
Where lay a vagrant dog in some extremity.
There he knelt and set his cup upon the ground.
The dog rolled up his eyes to see what man
Had come to succor him,
But could not lift its head to drink.
Seeing this, the Master dipped his fingers in his cup
And spread a trace of water round its mouth.
"I beseech you, Rabbi—
The darkness falls,
And others wait for us.
We can no longer tarry here."
At this the Master looked up an chided me:
"Shall I withdraw the cup
I've set before this suffering dog
And leave it here to languish in the dark.
Do you think my heart that small?
Verily, I tell you I will stay with him until he drinks,
And if he dies we'll stay to make a grave for him.
Retire to the well to wait and watch

Till I have done what I have come to do,"
And with these words
He turned away
And gently laid his hand
Upon the creature's head
And began to pray.

I grew weary waiting by the well,
Listening to the murmur of his voice
Steal through the night and settle in my ears,
But just before I lost my fight to stay awake
It came to me:
It was a blanket he was making of his prayers
To place upon the dog,
To let it know that it was loved.
He knew the water from the well was not enough.

Suddenly I awoke to find him standing over me:
"Was it too much to ask you to stay awake and watch?
Come, the dog has taken water and is resting now.
Tomorrow he will rise and walk.
But you have rested long enough.
Here. Take my hand.
I'll help you to your feet."

We walked in silence for awhile,
Until at length I took the Master's sleeve,
And when he turned to look at me
I said to him:
"Rabbi,
For all the miles we have walked together

Continued

And all that I have heard you say,
And all that I have seen you do,
I did not know until this night
The fullness of your Love."

....

One night as I pursued my solitary way
I came upon a crowd of hateful men
Closed in around some "object" of their scorn,
And though they didn't carry stones,
Still they stood there stoning him with words.
The terror-stricken soul,
Caught in this sudden torrent of abuse,
Had fallen to his knees
And folded to the ground,
His hands held over his ears.
"Stop this!" I roared,
And without a thought
I pushed my way through backs of faceless men,
Knelt down
And took the helpless creature in my arms.
And there we took the hurled "stones" together
Until the mocking stopped
And they moved back
And disappeared into the night.
Was then the creature
Lifted up his eyes to me
And what I saw in them
Astonished me!!
And what he saw in mine
Astonished him!!

Old barn,
Dilapidated,
No longer useful as a barn,
Solitary now,
A stark remainder,
And a reminder to passers by
That time has no friends,
That decrepitude
Awaits all
Who endure long enough.
Yet when the Sun is just right,
Or the Moon,
It comes alive again,
Becomes Beautiful and True again,
And is therefore still useful
To one who sees the Light
Falling on it
Or through it
As I do now
This winter morn
Standing off from it
Alone in the snow.

....

While many find their larger meaning
In some farfetched and fantastic
Religious mythology,
Some few others "find themselves"
By getting lost
In the farfetched and fantastic
"Biography" of the Cosmos!!

"So beautifully the moonlight falls
Upon this quiet grove of trees, Rabboni.
And look how lovely lay the shadows
Cast upon the ground.
Can we tarry here awhile
And just be still
And hearken to the Wordlessness of God?"

"How dear you are, my Beloved.
Your eyes see Beauty everywhere they look,
And your heart is always open to its Blessedness.
Truly, our spirits are not separate one from the other.
Come, let me fold my arms around you.
I want to feel the warmth of your body
And the beat of your heart—-
Now let me look at you.
So lovely you are,
My dear companion soul!
Would that you could see
The quiet spill of moonlight on your face,
And how it moves about so softly in your eyes,
Like tiny candles burning.
Oh how I wish this hour would slow and stop,
And never start again,
That we could stay the Moon in the Sky,
And be together always so,
Just as we are now,
Here in this blessed place.
But alas, my Love,
We know the hour cometh and cometh soon
When I must finish

What I've come to do."
"Hush, Rabboni,
Speak not of it tonight
Tonight let us pretend—
Forget for just tonight
The sword that soon will fall and sunder us.
No more of this—no not another word!
Cleave to me, Rabboni,
Let me cleave to you—
As if this were our final hour—
As if our final hour would never come."

....

Christians and Muslims and Buddhists, etc.
All await the "second coming,"
While the Jews patiently
Await the "first."
But it seems to me more likely than not
That the Hope of Mankind
Has never been here before—
And is not coming?

....

If you Love me and do not judge me
Then you Accept me as I am,
And if you Love and do not judge anything
Then you Accept God as God IS.

As water vapors in the sky
Begin to freeze and crystalize
Around a particle of careless dust,
Physics picks up its tiny tools
And begins to craft the bonding molecules,
And Chance leans near
And whispers some sweet nothing
Into the snowflake's ear.

....

A little girl asks her mother:
"Mommy, why is a Snowman always a man?
Couldn't' we make a Snow woman, instead?"
The mother smiled and said,
"Well, Sweetheart, somebody just imagined it that way,
And that somebody was no doubt a man.
If you would rather make a snow woman,
We could certainly do that."
"Oh, could we really, Mommy?
And I was wondering something else:
Why is God always a man?
I think I would rather have a Mother God.
Could we do that too, Mommy?
Could we make God a woman?"
The mother looked up, smiled broadly,
Then kneeled down and gave her daughter a big hug.
"I don't see why not, Sweetheart."
If we can imagine a Snow woman
I don't see why
We can't imagine a Mother God."

He had lost his wife some months ago,
And when I talked with him
And asked how he was getting on,
He looked at me
And I could see the answer in his eyes:
"Oh, my good friend,
I'm doing well enough, I guess,
But her absence is always Present."

....

If the placid and compassionate Buddha
Came upon a ferocious brute
Savagely raping a woman along some byway,
Even as her terrified children huddled in a shadow crying,
I like to think he would not close his eyes
And OM the Brahman,
But would pick up a rock or solid plank
And strike the raging brute on the head.
And I believe he would.
And I believe the gentle Rabbi
Would do the same.

....

We had to be "human"
To survive the perils of this world,
And now we have to become less "human"—
Or Perish from the Earth.

She doesn't judge or condemn—ANYTHING,
Believes that every event on this earth
And every event in all the far heavens
And in the heavens beyond them
Are "acts of god."
But this little "act of god" that she is
Would fight to the death
The little "acts of god" that others are
Who are bent on establishing
Ignorance and brutality on this earth—
In the name of an ignorant and brutal god!

....

When I look up into the night sky
And see the Moon up there,
As I do now,
I think of the shared experience
I am having
With every other pair of eyes
That ever looked up
To see and Wonder it,
From the first proto humans
To the likes of Buddha and Jesus
And Joan of Arc...
And for a magic moment or two
I get this strange feeling
I'm seeing the Moon through their Eyes,
And even stranger
I get this feeling
That for a magic moment or two
They're seeing the moon through mine!

When I awoke to pains in my chest last night
And thought I might be dying,
Instead of being overwhelmed with fear
And seeing my life flash by before my eyes,
I found myself composed in a Starry Wonderland
And it was so Beautiful and Still
And I felt so—
"Welcome."
And I had the sensation
That I had been absent for awhile—
And was returning.
And then I fell back to sleep...
And woke in my bed,
My heart at peace.

....

Consider this:
The Cosmos had a birthing moment
And an infancy
And has been developing
And maturing ever since
And will grow old and die someday.
You could almost say it's Alive!
And if you look at us
And our biological life cycle
And our consciousness of the Cosmos
You could almost say—could say in fact—
It IS Alive—
In us!!

Decided this morning
To wash the large burgundy bath towel
I use as bedding for my cat,
Which I did, by hand.
It promised to be a Sunny day—
And warm for December—
So I hung it on the back clothesline
Using three wooden clothes pins.
That done I stood back and smiled
Thinking that neighbors would notice
And find it odd to see
A lone burgundy towel
Hanging out on a line—
In December!
An hour later
I decided to walk to the grocery store,
And one block down
And three blocks over
A bird call turned my eyes
To someone's back yard,
And I literally stopped in my tracks
And stood in stupid astonishment,
For there—
Hanging alone on the clothesline,
Secured by three wooden clothes pins—
A large burgundy bath towel!!!
(I'm not sure
what to make of coincidences like this.
Some think they come to us as Cosmic couriers
Or "wonderful counsellors,"
But I'm inclined to think

That every now and then
We just get pranked
By the Improbability Principle.)

....

Many times in my life
Have I had reason
To recall
The wisdom
Of an early 19th century Hasidic Master—Reb Bunim:
"A person should have two pieces of paper,
One in each pocket,
To be used as necessary.
On one should be written:
'For me was the world created.'
And on the other:
'I am dust and ashes.'"

....

I have never walked to my car
After a funeral service
Without feeling
That I had just witnessed
The memorializing
Of perhaps the most remarkable
And beloved human being
Who ever walked the face of the earth.

....

Every day is the end of the world as we know it.

A stray dog,
Part of a family now,
Four little kids
Standing by the curb
With their mother—
Suddenly the pup
Darts into the street...
Blackie,
Our little foundling
That we loved and needed so much,
And who just as much loved and needed us,
Crushed to death before our eyes.
I still see the back of the car
Hurtling down the street,
The careless sound of it,
The sight and smell
Of the dark exhaust,
And I still see Blackie
Mangled there near the curb,
A broken, bloody thing—
Like the heart of the little boy
Who saw it happen—
And the heart of the old man
Who remembers.

(Strange how some memories,
Long ago laid to rest,
At times can quicken
With all the emotional force
Of a current event.)

You have been sitting alone in a theater
For what seems like an eternity
Watching a large black screen.
Finally, a point of light appears in the center
Then quickly swells into a small round density,
Expanding now into a ghostly ball
And diffusing into a glowing ring of Light.
You notice that as it begins to fill the screen
The outer and the center mist of it
Become progressively less dense,
And now the thin outer part of the Mistiness
Begins to move off the screen
And the center becomes a growing vacancy.
Finally the last of the points recede,
Leaving the black screen as you found it,
A large dark expanse of nothingness.
You continue sitting alone in the theater
For what seems like an eternity,
And then you stand up and leave.

....

I feel the Eternal
Out there pressing to get in,
And feel it inside,
Bursting to get out.
What am I to make of myself?
And "You," Eternal Mystery,
Storming my castle walls,
What am I to make of "You?"

Darkness.
Desperate for Light.
Pupils
Dilate to the outer rim.
True Brightness.
Pupils
Tighten to a needle's point,
All but blinding me.
Therefore I grope.

....

A hare sits nibbling on a clump of clover.
Suddenly, she lifts her head—
Freezes—
Eyes, ears, nose on high alert!
"Uh oh! That's no squirrel.
What the devil is it?
And what's it up to?"
She watches with alarm but fascination
As the strange creature
Jumps about erratically,
Falls, rolls,
Lays on its back,
Then explodes into the air again
Twisting and turning all the while.
"It must be overfull of mirth,
Or has eaten some loco weed,"
She thinks.
"But I don't' think it's seen me yet.
Better remain completely still.
Maybe in a moment

It will bolt away and be gone."
She has no idea that the creature
In fact HAS seen her,
And she is unaware
That it is clowning closer and closer,
And before she has any idea
What is happening
The cute but cunning weasel
Has pounced on her,
Coiled his lean body around her
And clamped its jaws
Around the back of her neck.

....

Vaucoulers,
Near the Gate of France,
A very large and very old lime tree.
Your guide tells you
That local legend has it
That Joan of Arc
Once tied her horse to a branch of that tree—
(No doubt a stripling then).
And standing there,
Hearing that story,
You feel a sudden backward rush of time
And hear the whinny of a horse,
And for a split second
You are there
And witness the slender Maid
Checking the bridle of her mount.

Every impingement on our senses
Is a Revelation,
And thanks to Reason and rigor,
Science continues to make sense of those Revelations,
Turning our Wonder
Into Understanding,
And our Darkness into Light,
And this special Knowing
This gradual uncovering
Of the Truth of things,
Brings us Nearer.

....

We owe our lives to the death of stars.

....

God is not an accountant.

....

The Cosmos,
Neither malicious nor benevolent,
Has yet evolved an organism
That is both!!
And that organism,
Both malicious and benevolent,
Is unable to imagine
A Cosmos which is neither.

I cannot teach you how to Love
Until I've taught you
How to Forgive.
And I cannot teach you how to Forgive
Until I've taught you
How to Love.
Maybe if I could just teach you
That behind every outcome of the Cosmos
Is a Trail of Understanding
That traces back to the beginning of time
And that every expression of the Cosmos
Is the perfect consequence
Of all that preceded it—
Maybe then I could teach you
How necessary it is to Love
And not to judge.

....

Two men
Sit wondering the contents of a mysterious box
Which they found in a dark place.
Unable to access the box
They conjecture endlessly
What might be in it,
But to no avail,
Until one man suggests to the other:
Maybe we should start thinking
Inside the box.

The closed mind is a kind of box—or "safe,"
Which is hard to break into
And just as hard to break out of.
An open mind is also a kind of box
But there are windows in it—
And a door.
(In all fairness,
Those who have an open mind
Don't spend a lot of time in front of the windows
And rarely venture out
Or welcome strangers in.)

....

The danger of thinking outside the box
Too long and too hard
Is that you may reach that point of urgency
Where you are no longer able
To think inside the box!

....

A mind should expand to fill the space outside of it.

....

Peering through the Hubble telescope
Into the deep field of the Cosmos
I can't help but feel,
In some very profound way,
That I'm not observing—
But introspecting!!

I am a tree.
I push my roots
Deep into the ground,
Grasping at the earth
And holding tight;
An anchorage for me.
And lift my arms,
Reaching up with all my might
To take the Sun in my hands.
And when the planet turns
The Star of Day from sight
My branches strain
To touch the Stars of Night—
Thus do I have an anchorage
In Earth and Heaven both.

....

When I feel around the walls
Of the dark box I'm in
I feel only a surface that is curved!
And even stranger than that,
The curve is curving out!
Away from me!
As if I'm outside the Roundness
Of the box I'm in!

....

I require God to be the way God IS
And God requires me to be the way I AM

The "Kingdom of God" is within us,
Though it's not a kingdom really,
For kingdoms have a king—
More like a "wild kingdom,"
But it's not really wild,
For it evolves with perfect integrity
Ever striving for a Harmony
It can never achieve
And searching for a Peace
It can never know.
And just to think
That we emerged from it,
And are, in some elemental way,
Destined to be eternal with it!
Oh! The Wonder of that!
That the Cosmos is Alive
And has Dreamed itself Awake—
In Us!!

....

But for Stars
That perished long ago,
There'd be no Earth
Or Sky
Or surge of sea
No rain or snow
Nor any we
To trace our ancestry
To Stars that perished
Long ago.

All the Beauty of Tomorrow
Awaits the passing
Of what is Beautiful—
Today.

....

I watched a Leopard at the zoo today
And when he wandered near
And turned to look at me,
I could see in his eyes
That he no longer remembered
Who he was,
Or how it was
That he had come to this despairing place,
And as he turned
And slouched away
I had this strange feeling
That when the Leopard looked at me
He had seen in my eyes
The same thing.

....

We need to see our lives,
Not only from the inside looking out—
From the Deep inside—
But from the outside
Looking in!
From the Way outside!!

When I was a little boy
I used to hear strange sounds
Coming from the Attic of my House
(Which haunted but never frightened me)
And often I would sit with my ear
Soft against the door
And just Listen...
Oh, I would hear all the ordinary things—
The creaks and scratching sounds,
The occasional soft thud or shuffling about
And now and then a quiet snap
As from the breaking of a dry twig.
"Something is making those sounds," I'd think,
And wonder what?
Sometimes I would hear—
Or imagine I heard—
More unusual things.
One time I thought I heard a hushed voice
Whispering things I couldn't understand—
Some kept secret maybe,
Or profession of love,
Or a prayer,
And once a wisp of tinkling sounds
That seemed to come from a wind chime
Hanging in the backyard
Of some other world
Or from an old music box
Wrapped in a heavy quilt
And packed away in a trunk.
How I wanted to go up there!
To find out what was making

Those Strange and Enchanting sounds,
But for some reason
The door had been sealed shut
And I never got to climb those stairs.
Well, I grew up
And have made my way through the years
And have grown old,
But still at the end of every day
When I lay down and close my eyes,
I always lean my ear
Soft against that Attic door
And Listen...
And Wonder myself to sleep,
Perhaps in sleep
To dream myself a passage
Up the attic stairs.

....

Some say of Beauty, "She's a fraud, a lie!
A fairy queen we see when all is well
But poofs! to pixie dust when all goes wrong
And leaves behind no lasting Truth to tell."

Seems sometimes so—but what if Truth itself
Is Beauty—even when it horrifies!
Perhaps when we turn eyes away and cringe
We miss the Beauty, even in what crucifies!

Sometimes I break down and weep.
I cannot tell you why.
Some past sorrow that I keep,
Perhaps,
Or treasured joy,
Starts up in me
And I begin to cry.

Sometimes I think
It's more than that—
That what wells up in me
Is that dread certainty
That we,
Our Earth and Sun
And every turning galaxy
Will someday
Consummate and die
And all things Beautiful
Will pass away.
Maybe that is why
Sometimes my heart gives way
And I begin to cry.

Still that should not defeat the Beauty of the day

....

We are self conscious marionettes
With a mind of our own.

God is the Pointing Finger,
Pointing everywhere,
And all at once,
As if appointing everything,
And at the other end of the Pointing Finger—
Is the Finger—Pointing.

....

The Mystic Depot.
All the tracks in all the lands
Lead out from it
And all the tracks in all the lands
Return to it.
Every departing "train" arrives at this destination.

....

A little girl runs away
And gets lost in the Wilderness.
One day
Someone who loves her
Discovers her hiding
In a little hollow of dense undergrowth
And kneels and takes her in his arms,
And when, with tears in his eyes,
He asks her,
"Oh why did you run away, my little angel.
You worried me to death!!"
With tears in her eyes, she answered:
"Because I wanted you to find me."

"God" grants "free will" to men
Knowing in advance
How they will choose.
Still we go on choosing,
Free-willing our way
To the place
Where we are destined to arrive.

....

A densely wooded hill,
A young boy,
Climbing by himself,
Exploring—Searching.
Higher and higher he climbs...
And still higher.
"I'm so tired," he mutters,
But he climbs on.
Finally the ground begins to level out
And he finds himself entering a small clearing
And looks around wide eyed,
Surprised and gladdened
To find such a unexpected place.
And then he sees it!
And it takes his breath away.
"It isn't possible!" he cries.
"It just can't be! But there it is!"
Suddenly his legs give way
And he becomes a heap on the ground
Where he slumps in wonder watching
While his whole being
Rings like a great bell

Which has just been struck!
Then suddenly it is gone—
Just like that,
Leaving him alone in the clearing,
Still trembling inside.
"Oh, but I can never tell anyone what I saw," he laments,
"For no one would ever believe me."

And though many times after that day,
He climbed back to that clearing,
The wonder that he saw never appeared again,
And though he never told anyone about it.
His heart still rings
With the exquisite sound of what he saw.

....

We are little Fictions
Believing ourselves True.
And little Prisoners
Believing ourselves Free.
Strange for a Fictitious Prisoner
To believe such things.

....

God is not the Magician
Pulling the rabbit out of the black hat—
God is the Magician
Inside the black hat
Pushing the rabbit out!

The Beauty of the Universe
Lies in the Initial Mystery of its Genesis
The Uncertainty Principle of its infancy
The Certainty Principle of its Evolution
And the Mystery of its destiny.

....

We both leaned forward,
And our heads came together,
And we stood there like that
For some long moments,
Enveloped in an awful stillness,
Each in a desperation all his own.

Finally we came apart,
And I looked at him,
My eyes wide with horror and dismay,
My heart struck by a bolt.

"You know I love you, Rabbi,
But I cannot do as you ask.
Ask me to cut off my hand
Or claw out my eyes
Or to go and live with the lepers.
Ask me even to hang myself from a tree.
These things I would do for you.
But not that."

And then he took me by my arms,
And held me steady in his hands:

"I know you love me,
And surely you know
The measure of my love for you.
I ask you to take this cup
Because only one
Who loves with his whole heart
Can drink from it.
I know you will not break faith with me."

He went on to share with me
The terrible shape of things to come
And of the Beauty
In the terrible shape of them...

Then sound from the other room
Turned his head that way,
And he took me by the hand:

"Look, the table is set.
We are waited for.
Come, let us be brave
And suffer together
What each of us must suffer apart.
We will come together again
When it is finished.
God be with you, beloved friend."

He then leaned close
And kissed me on the cheek.

Just outside my house—
An erratic scratchy sound
Coming from above my head.
The gutter.
(Covered with a latticed guard
To keep out leaves).
A small bird
Somehow found a way in
Unable to find a way out.
Frantically traipsing back and forth
Up and down the gutter length—
Scratching out his desperation.
How like the trapped bird
The trapped man
Who lifts the latticework
And watches
As the small bird flies away.

....

(An alternate musing about Judas and his relationship with Jesus):

Look at him sitting there
So satisfied and sure of himself,
Smiling warmly at the soft murmurings
Of those who wait on him,
Seeming to thrive under their fawning care—
And now allowing that unclean woman
To let down her hair
In front of us
And put her hands on him.

How wanton she is
And how he welcomes her attentions.
Is this the man
To establish the New Jerusalem?
And is this the man
That teaches us to sacrifice for the poor
Who now allows the spikenard
To be lavished upon himself?
The money parted with to buy
That pint of perfumed spice
Could feed five hungry children for a year!
Is this truly the one we have waited for?
Is this God come to us?

Look how Peter turns his back to him
And how a cloud darkens
Even the face of John—

John—remembering now the Baptist John,
And how he himself came to wonder
If this man Jesus was the One...

During Passover in Jerusalem next week.
There will I do what I must do.
God guide and strengthen me.

....

You can be "free,"
Or you can be close to God,
But you can't be both.

Pilate: That is some scheme you suggest, Joseph.
I like it. It is daring and dangerous...
And a hundred pieces of gold
Is a handsome sum!
Even to the Roman Prefect of Judaea.
Is this man so dear to you?
But I'm afraid the matter is settled;
The scourging and execution is tomorrow.

Joseph: I know the plan is desperate
And not without risk, Prefect,
But a man of your eminence and authority,
And a man of my trust and discretion,
Could make it work.
I don't suppose I can explain to you why,
But yes, Prefect, he is that dear to me.
I will make it two hundred!
A thoughtful silence comes between them.

Pilate: Make it three, Joseph.
And I will help you save your friend.
Either way, I will be rid of him,
Your High Priests will be satisfied (and none the wiser),
And I will be enriched by 300 Aurei!

But just to be clear, Joseph:
Though I consider you a friend and a confidant,
If this man Jesus is ever seen in Judaea again
He will be trussed up to the column,
Savagely beaten,
Then promptly crucified—for the second time!

And you will be arrested
And charged with treason.
Is that clear?

Joseph: It is. I will keep him out of sight,
And as soon as arrangements can be made
We two will board a merchant ship
And sail to a distant land
Never to return.
You have my word, Prefect.

Pilate: Then we are agreed—
Though I will miss a man such as you, Joseph.

Now give me your hand
And come share a cup of wine with me
While we make sure our plan.

....

We can learn from the evolution of matter
And from the evolution of Life
That the Cosmos is a restless and contentious place,
That Conflict is the Rule
And Conflict resolution is the Way,
The Way always leading back to the Rule.
It is a game played out on the field of Time and Space
And ends when the last of all conflicting players
Expire on the Field
And the Field itself plays out.

Take away all the miracles
And all the parables
And the beatitudes
And all the fulfillments of scripture
And all the prophesies of things to come,
And all the rest,
But leave the two great commandments—
And the third
Which follows from the first two:
"Judge not."
It would be enough.

....

Not long after the daily executions,
As I struggled up a narrow path,
Lamenting the violent ways
Of gods and men alike,
The treachery and callousness of both,
I came upon a wretched soul
Slumped against a tree,
Convulsing in pain,
His heart draining out of his eyes,
More alone and despairing,
It seemed to me,
Than an animal caught in a trap
Or a man affixed to a cross.
I could not pass and leave him there like that,
Tortured and forsaken as he was,
And so drew near and placed my hand on him:
"I am here," was all that I could think to say,
Then took him in my arms

And held him close,
As a father would hold close a dying son.
And when his torment shuddered out
And I could feel him coming back to life,
I stepped back,
Took the flask of water from my side
And held it to his lips.
After he had drunk from it,
He raised his eyes and searched my face.

Then, as I wished him peace
And turned to go,
I noticed a length of rope
Fall from his hand.

....

Cargo: Golden Records,
Telling of a Planet
And of the diversity of Life there,
Highlighting the culture of intelligent beings,
A kind of "time capsule"
A "note in a bottle" sent adrift
In the Cosmic Sea
Perhaps many light years later
To "wash ashore" somewhere,
Likely arriving not as an announcement,
But as a memorial.

On Good Friday
It is Judas we condemn and despise,
And we take little note
That, when trouble came,
All the rest of the disciples,
Cowered in fear
And disappeared into the shadows.
It is strange to me
That among those
Who had followed Jesus
Through the years
And had walked with him
And broke bread with him
And sat at his feet and marveled at his words
And witnessed the miraculous power of his love—
Not one had faith in him enough
Or was brave enough
Or loved him enough
To stand by him
When Danger hemmed him in.
I find that strange.

....

What was evidence enough for Doubting Thomas
That Jesus had been resurrected from the dead
Would not have been evidence enough for me.
When Jesus showed me the crucifixion wounds
I would have said,
"That only proves you have been wounded and are alive.
It does not prove that you were ever dead."

If a person could improve his stature
By standing on his toes
And reaching for something far above his head,
By this time of my life
I would be breathing the vacuum of deep space—
Which I am,
And have stars in my hair,
Which I do.

....

The Cosmos
Is elemental and evolutionary
And marvelous,
But before evolving contemplative creatures
It was unconscious of itself.
It was not seen or wondered
Or understood or appreciated.
It just Was.
How extraordinary
That the Cosmos,
In giving birth to "us,"
In a very real sense,
Has given birth to itself!!
Think of that!!
Before "us"
The Cosmos had no eyes
Nor a mirror to look into:
We are those eyes!
We are that mirror!

A woman falls on knees
And cries out in despair:
"God, can you ever forgive me?"
And a mighty grief tears at God's heart,
And he takes the woman in his arms
And says to her:
Dear grieving woman,
Lift up your eyes to me:
How can I make you understand
That there is nothing to forgive?
Sin is a word without meaning to me,
For I am not a God of judgment,
But a God of Understanding,
And nothing you have ever thought or done
Has ever angered or offended me.

Out of my own emptiness
Have I emerged,
And out of my own fullness
Have I put Life in you,
And I alone am responsible for you.
The "fault" you find in yourself
Is not yours,
And the "guilt" you feel
Is not your own.
Can you Understand that?
And though it was never my intention
That you should come to harm
You have,
And in hurting you
I have done an injury to myself.

And so we suffer together.
But if you could only Understand
That I Am that I Am,
And could not be other than I Am,
And that I have brought you forth out of myself
To be just as you Are,
Then you can heal
And I can heal with you.
Can you do that?

Dear grieving woman,
I wonder if you can know
That I have Understood and Loved you
From the beginning of time,
And that long after all the flowers have wilted in the field
And all the stars have fallen from the sky
And time itself has come to an end,
I will hold you blameless in my arms
As I do now.

....

Blake asked the hard question:
"Did he who make the lamb make thee?"
(And the answer has to be, "Yes.")
Then Blake judged: How "dare" he?
Showing, I think,
That he had a hard time understanding
That "God" was not more like him.

Asteroid impacts, Earthquakes, Floods, Conflagrations,
Epidemics, Volcanoes, Droughts, Tidal Waves...etc.—
All cause horrific damage and death and suffering,
But they are all
Unintentional consequences of the evolving Cosmos—
All "Acts of God."
And the physical and personal sufferings
Of every creature on the Earth
As they struggle to survive
Are likewise all unintentional consequences,
All "Acts of God."

....

The Hubble Telescope has lifted the veil on the face of the Cosmos,
But we are still trying to mind out what is in its heart—
If it has one.

....

It is either the case
That an unconscious and mindless Cosmos
Has evolved a creature
That is both conscious and mindful
Or that the conscious and mindful creature
Is the Great Work
Of a conscious and mindful Cosmos.

....

We are able to forgive ourselves
And each other
When we are able to forgive "God."

You have heard it said
That to understand is to forgive,
But I say unto you
Blessed are they
Who forgive without understanding.

....

As we stagger through the horror
Of this soulless place
Where even the light from the Sun
Is blackened by a cloud of soot
We find no refuge from our despair,
Which is unrelenting and profound,
But as we shuffle along,
Toward the place where the cloud is made,
We notice a woman looking up,
And her face seems lit
By a Brightness in the sky,
And we wonder how it's possible
That from the sooty cloud
Rays of light have broken through
And fallen on this woman's face?
And then we realize
That the Light on her face
Is coming from inside,
From a Sun in her own private Sky
Which is blue
And where no soot is,
And we look down at our shoes,
And weep.

From the Science of Cosmic evolution
And the principles governing the evolution of life
We learn that Beauty is the outcome
Of a long history of violence,
That Peace is only a very brief interlude,
That Love and Hate
Are chemical reactions,
And Good and Evil
Simply neural concoctions—
And yet,
Though the Evolutionary Cosmos
Is Violent!!
And Unforgiving!!
And Indifferent!!
And Inexorable!!
It is also ferociously Enchanting!!

....

It's hard to see ourselves as we are,
And still love ourselves,
And just as hard to see others as they are
And still love them.
But the hardest thing
Is to see "God" as "God" IS
And still love "God."

....

Reality is not subject to my approval.
Nor is the Truth of Things.

We are emotional
And morally dualistic,
Unlike "God."
And some of us are sensitive and compassionate,
Unlike "God."
And unlike "God,"
Some of us are cruel.
A few of us are indifferent
And just don't care—
Like "God."

....

Reality is the evolving face of Possibility.

....

Two things the Universe abhors:
Chaos—
And Perfection.
It has but one compelling urge—
To Evolve—To Become!!

....

Woman sitting at table.
Old cat on table wants down.
Peers over the edge.
Too risky, it thinks.
Woman turns her chair
And posts up a thigh,
Giving the old cat a "leg down."

Behind the deserted barn,
Lying alone in the dirt and filth,
His collar tight around his neck,
The chain to the collar
Held by an iron stake
Driven deep into the ground,
A once playful and beautiful dog
Now struggles to make sense of things.
He is alone and despairing,
And can't understand
Why he has been abused and neglected
And fastened here in this forsaken place.
He doesn't understand cruelty
And he's not sure he wants to.
He just lies there—
His eyes empty of hope or care,
Trying not to think
Trying not to feel.
When it gets dark again
He will lift up his eyes to the sky.
He doesn't know why he does this.
Maybe just because
The specks of light out there
Make him think of some other place
Than here.
He will wait for sleep
And when sleep comes
Maybe he will dream again of days that were
When his small world made sense
And all he knew was tenderness and joy,
Knowing that such dreams as these

Will only make his waking hours worse.
Better not to dream, he thinks,
Or if to dream,
Better not to wake.
He looks over at the iron stake
Driven deep into the dirt
And stares at it
And wonders if the ground
Knows how to hurt.
Then follows the chain
Back to where he lies
And wonders if anybody cares.

....

After the slaughter of the Mountain People
"One Tin Soldier Rides Away."
But who is he?
Where does he ride to?
Can he ride away far enough
To hide from his shame,
Or his cowardice,
Or his profound remorse?
And the last of the Mountain People,
How does he survive his own passivity,
His own guilt,
His own disillusionment.
What thoughts are his
Who now sits alone on the ground
Amid the bodies of his kith and kin
The broken pieces of the Treasure Stone
Piled in his lap?

I gathered up all the pain and suffering
Of every creature who ever lived
And took it to "God"
And laid it at his feet.
"Why?" I cried.
And "God" went out
And gathered up all the Beauty and Joy
In the world,
And brought it back
And held it in his hands:
"It was the only way," he said.

....

When I came upon a very old man
Creaking slowly and painfully
Down the road of his life,
So slumped over
He could no longer lift his head
To look me in the eyes,
I said to him:
"Excuse me—
If you have a moment
I wonder if you could tell me
The most important lesson
You have learned from your long life."
He stopped
Carefully tilted his head a little to one side,
Angled his eyes up to me,
And said with deadly soberness:
"Young man, don't ever let yourself get this old."

Life is a Glad Journey—
And a Trail of Tears.
If it were not both,
It would not be either.

....

"God" is not obliged
To be the way
That men imagine "God."
But men are bound
To be the way
That "God" imagined them.

....

On her journey
She came upon an abyss
Around which there was no way.
So she descended into it.
Stories are still told
By those who dwell on the other side
That once a woman
Climbed out of the abyss
Who glowed in the dark!

....

His thoughts were too big
To fit into his head
And his heart not big enough
To hold his sensitivities.

A man peers into a looking glass
And studies his reflection,
And it occurs to him
With sudden clarity—
That he IS a Reflection.

....

I come upon a Door.
There is a sign on it.
"Beware!" it says.
"Do not open.
Death to any
Who would enter here."
I look back over the way I have come,
Then open Door.

....

I couldn't say for sure it was a weed,
Tall and stately as it was
And standing there among the other weeds
As if it didn't quite belong,
But I dismissed the thought.
I was hot and tired
And wanted those weeds gone.
And so I sprayed the little corner spot
With potent herbicide
And went about my other chores.
The coming days proved that the spray
Was good at what it did,
For all the weeds turned brown and died—

Except the tall and stately one.
Oh, it suffered greatly from the lethal spray
But fought for life.
"I will not die," it said.
"I cannot die
Until I've done what I have come to do."
I let it struggle there like that
Alone among the brown remains
And kept an eye on it
As summer days turned into weeks.
And by and by the topmost part of it
Greened up again.
And then this morning,
There upon the highest reaching stem,
Wet with dew,
Four heart-shaped petals
Opened in a lemon-yellow bloom
Beautiful enough
To forgive even the man
Who tried to murder it.

....

When men dig up
Or cause some other calamity
To a colony of ants,
The ants regard it as a natural disaster—
Or an "act of god,"
Which,
Broadly speaking,
It is.

When you forgive yourself
You forgive the world—
Without a sacrificial lamb!!

....

Broken Goose,
Earth bound,
Picking her solitary way
Around the pond,
Puzzling her incapacity,
Wondering her aloneness,
Her heart a crippled thing
Like the wing that sags on her side.
She longs to struggle up
Into the sky again
With others of her kind,
Again with them to push her face into the wind
And leave behind this lonely resting place.
"Oh, to fly again," she cries.

When she hears
The honking geese sail over her,
She lifts her head,
High as her long neck will reach,
And answers with a sigh.

But after they have sailed away
And the sound of them has passed,
She looks about at the grass and the water
And the far trees and the tall sky
And travels back in time

And brings to life again
All their many flights
And time together on the ground,
And something in her
Fills with gratitude and joy,
And she is not afraid
Of the eyes
Watching from the brush.

....

Oh, those sudden overwhelming bouts
Of exhilaration!
When you step outside and look about
And every sense
Opens to the natural world
And you are utterly overcome
With the extraordinary Consciousness
That you are truly and fully Alive!!
That you are not only in the Presence
Of the All of Everything,
But are infused with it
And inseparable from it!!
Oh, what a Quickening it is!!
As if the Universe
Has suddenly decided
To birth itself all over again—
In you!!

I see you looking at that walking stick
Standing in the corner there.
I cut it from an Evening Primrose plant
Which chose to send down roots
Among the weeds
Which grew beside my neighbor's fence,
The four foot length of it
Not half the height it grew to be.
You're right to say
It looks like sturdy wood,
And if I let you take it in your hand
You'd find it has the feel and heft and strength of wood.
But it's a Primrose stem alright.
I'll vouch for that.

I wonder if you've heard about a man
Who stuck his walking stick into the ground
And overnight it grew into a Hawthorne tree—
The Holy Thorn of Glastonbury,
I think it's called.
No, it wasn't Merlin,
Some merchant from the holy land,
If I remember right.

Well, that took place two thousand years ago.

Now I don't claim
That if you took that walking stick
And stuck it in the ground
That it would spring to life again—
Wouldn't surprise me though if it did.

I can tell you this:
Months ago,
When Death came to take that Primrose plant
It just plain refused to go,
Stern as you please
Told Death it wasn't finished yet.
And every day throughout the August month
It blessed the world with fresh new blooms
Lovely as the eye can bear to see.

And in a very special way,
Standing there in the corner,
Cut down and trimmed,
Just as you see it now,
It's still Alive!
Why I can still see the yellow flowers
Birthing on the stems I've cut away—

Oh, don't look at me as if I'm daft.
Can I help it if my heart has eyes?

....

No sweeter music ever heard
By ears that hear
And hearts that long
Than from the throat
Of some small bird
Who jewels the break of day
With song.

"This too shall pass,"
Words that help to get you through
The heartbreaks and the bouts of pain,
But Oh! The rue of them
When Beauty takes you by the hand
And leads you down a flowered lane.

....

When a little boy
Comes across a small bottle
Buried in the sand,
He pries it loose and lifts it up.
The glass is clear
And he can see an agitated figure trapped inside
Pressing the palms of his hands
Against the bottle walls,
And when he looks closely,
He sees that the figure is a little boy,
And when he holds the bottle even closer
He becomes quite certain,
And quite astonished to discover,
That the little boy trapped inside the bottle
Is him!!
"How did I get in there?" he wonders
"And why have I washed ashore here?
And how can I get out?"
He tries to open the bottle
But the top seems fused to the bottle neck,
And tries to break the bottle with a rock,
But the glass will not break.
So he puts the bottle in his pocket

And takes it home with him
And hides it under his pillow.
But later,
When he takes it out
To wonder it some more,
He discovers the bottle is empty,
And somehow that alarms him,
And he goes to the window
And puts his palms against the glass
And looks out.

....

A crocodile suns itself
On the bank of a swampy glade
Digesting a large wading bird;
A butterfly lands on its back
And suns itself.

....

I know the poet saw Death
As the easy and pleasant passage
Out of the Garden,
But whenever I hear the line:
"Death is only an old door
Set in a garden wall"
I always imagine
An old man or woman
Standing at the door—
Preparing to enter.

We are taken from "Her" arms
When we are born,
And given a name,
And returned to "Her,"
When we die,
Without a name.
The Cosmic "Mother"
Rocks us to sleep in her arms
And we slumber off
To the sound of her breathing
And the soft beat of her heart...
...And in our sleep,
We dream ourselves awake
Into a world
Of perilous Beauty and Possibility
And wear ourselves out
Dancing and dodging our way
Through the rough and tumble of it all—
And finally we weary
And our eyes grow heavy
And we fall asleep again...

...And awake,
Warm in our Mother's arms,
To the sound of Her breathing
And the soft beat of Her heart.

....

If you don't believe in miracles you don't believe in anything

When the Master comes upon a woman
Slumped on the ground,
Trembling and weeping,
He goes to her:
"Why do you grieve so?" he asks.
"Oh," she sobs,
"The Darkness of this world
Has all but overcome the Light in me.
I don't know what else to do but grieve?"
"Here," he says,
"Take my hand.
Let me help you to your feet."
He then holds out his lamp:
"Across the way,
Lying in the shadows,
Is a small dog.
She is lost and alone,
And she is trembling.
Take this Light
And go to her."

....

I read somewhere once
That "depression is the inability to construct a future."
However, in the case of the very old
Or the very weak
Or of those who read History,
Depression is the ability—
TO construct a future.

Power line,
Stretched between two poles.
Perched on it,
A huge, broad-shouldered hawk.
Beside it,
Not two short feet away,
A small bird,
A sparrow maybe,
(Huge, broad-shouldered heart)
Both facing East,
Each perfectly still.
So strange to see them
Sitting there composed like that,
The greater bird seeming to know
It cannot threaten the lesser bird,
The lesser bird,
Seeming to know the same thing.
Then suddenly,
As if on cue,
The two birds turn their heads
To look each other in the eye!
Now I don't know
How much is understood
About the disposition of wild birds,
But it pleases me to think
That at this moment
Both of them would laugh out loud—
If they could.

A green leaf
Wearies on its stem,
Dries and turns a tired orange.
It tries to hang on
But at length a carefree gust
Takes hold
And tugs it free
And carries it off
To wherever it is leaves go
Once they weary on the stem
And a windy hand
Takes them from the tree.

....

"God" warned Adam and Eve
Of the danger and consequences
Of knowing good and evil,
Not because it would make them like God,
But because it would make them—
Unlike God.

....

What is a poet
But a kind of blacksmith
Who takes his heart out of the furnace,
Lays it on an anvil,
And beats it into words.

Outside
I am angular—
Lots of edges,
And sharp points—
But inside
I am soft and round,
Like the sound of an owl
Heard in the night
Or the glow from a lamplight
Seen through falling snow.

....

I come upon a man
Straining to keep aloft a great boulder
Which he holds in his arms
Balanced on the back of his neck.
"For gods sake, Good Man!
Why do you carry the weight of the world
On your shoulders like that?"
Sagging beneath the crush of it,
The man laments:
"Because I cannot close my Eyes."

....

I am not I, the I you see,
Just cleverly disguised as me.
I have a face and fingerprints,
But no identity.

As she shuffles along
In the haggard procession,
Her heart a pile of ashes now,
A mother
Looks down at the weariness
In her little girl's eyes
And pulls her close.
"We're almost there now, Zeisele.
Soon you will sleep in my arms,"
Then looks up at the dark obscenity
And watches her God go up in smoke.

....

Isn't it the worse kind of idolatry
To take a man and say of him:
"This man is God?"
Say of him
That he is understanding
That he is compassionate
That he is forgiving.
Say that he is a wise and wonderful man,
That you wish all men were like him,
Say even that you hope
That "God" is like this man,
But do not say of him:
"This man is God!"

I start and sit straight up in bed,
Wide-eyed,
My forehead wet,
My breathing quick—
"Was but an agitated dream," I think.
"I'm here, now,
Safe in my bed.
Was but an agitated dream."
Then suddenly—
I cannot tell you how I know—
But suddenly I know
I'm still asleep,
And in the middle of an agitated dream
Which finds me sitting upright in my bed
Imagining I'm awake.

....

Moving down a narrow lane
Alone
Late into a lonely night
I see a darkened figure up ahead
Approaching me.
I slow my pace,
And he,
Who sees a figure with a darkened face
Approaching him,
Slows his,
(Or "hers,"
As just as like the case may be,)
And then, as if on cue,
We both come still

And stand there motionless like that,
Two ciphers in the night,
Until, again as if on cue,
We turn about
And go our separate ways,
To separate rooms—
With doors which we keep locked.

....

Asked to write an essay about the nature of God,
One student,
Who had fallen in love
With the economy of thought and words,
Titled his essay:
"Beauty and the Beast,"
Then put his pencil down.

....

An old dog
Lies on the floor
And looks up at his Master
Asleep in his chair by the Fire.
The eyes of the old dog
Are full of wonder,
As they always are,
And his heart is full of longing,
As it always is.

A Carousel.
Calliope music.
Brightly colored lights.
The sound of laughter.
A little girl,
Rising and falling on a painted horse,
Her face full of joy,
Her heart free of care;
An old lady,
Alone on a park bench,
In the stillness
And the dark,
Watching what is no longer there
And listening to music
Which silenced long ago.

....

He stood there on his little Hill alone
And watched the greedy menace
Circle round this bit of higher, hallowed ground
Which he had dared to call his own and where
He chose to make his final stand,
And when the roar went up
By those ten score of savage men
Who thumped the ground with sharpened spears
And shook their mighty swords at him,
He stood there looking down
In pity at that cast of craven souls
That lacked the courage and the will
To stand alone upon a hill and die defending it.
And when they came to take him down—

This mighty mass of little men—
He stood triumphantly alone
And fought them like a demon loosed from hell,
And many widows made that happy day—
Before he fell.
And some there are that yet remain who say
That on a quiet night you still can hear
The battle cry of that lone man
Who stood his ground
And died upon his Hill.

....

Once in elementary school,
During the commotion of a fire drill,
An impulsive little boy
Filched a pocket book from a girl's locker—
Which in the excitement she had left open—
And after school,
Stealthing in an alleyway,
The young thief took the change he found inside
And dumped the purse in a trash can.
Many years later
The memory of his petty theft
Matured into a deep remorse
As he realized
That he had taken something
From that little girl
Far more precious than her purse,
And something from himself
That was not petty cash.

An old lady is sitting quietly in the park alone,
Her hands folded peacefully in her lap,
When a little girl approaches her.
　"What are you doing?" she asks.
"Oh, nothing at all," she says—
"Just being Still."
The little girl looks at her curiously.
　"What are you thinking about then?"
"Oh, but I'm not thinking—
I'm waiting for all my thoughts to fall asleep.
Then I just drift off."
　"Are you trying to fall asleep then?"
"Oh no, you see I only want my thoughts to fall asleep.
And when that happens
I feel as if I've fallen awake."
The little girl laughs.
　"You silly; you're already awake."
"I know I seem to be awake,
But as long as I'm thinking about things
I feel as if I'm asleep and missing something,
And when I stop thinking
Somehow I feel wide awake."
The little girl giggles again then puzzles some more:
　"But how do you stop thinking?
　I just don't see how you can."
"Well, young lady,
I bet you have a good imagination:
Now imagine you are in a rowboat,
And that "thinking" is like rowing,
Trying to control your little boat—to steer it.
Do you see what I mean?

Rowing, rowing, rowing,
Always rowing,
But when you just sit back
And bring your oars into your boat
It just drifts along with the current,
In a way becomes part of the River.
And becoming part of the River
Is what I call drifting off
Or falling Awake."
    "Oh, that sounds like such fun!
    Can I try?"
"Certainly you can.
But I have to tell you:
It's not as easy as you think.
The oars on your little boat
Don't want to come out of the water—
They want to row.
So getting them out and into your boat
Is sometimes hard to do."
    "What if I can't do it?"
"Well, then you just let go of them,
Fold your hands peacefully in your lap,
As I am doing now,
And just let yourself feel the River moving beneath you.
You might even forget you're in a boat.
That's when you know it's happened."
    "Know what's happened?"
"Well, Silly—
That's when you know you've fallen Awake!"
But just then the call of a girl's name—
    "Oh, there's my mommy,

Continued

I've got to go now.
I hope to see you again.
If you're not in the park
I'll look for you out in the River."
With this the little girl runs off giggling.

....

One evening on a venture out alone,
Hoping to find some solace in the quiet night,
I hear some movement coming from the wayside brush
And stop and look that way
When in the hush I hear a sigh,
And spy a clearing which I dare to step into
And where I see a half a dozen slaughtered men,
All lying there in gruesome disarray,
Just as they fell,
Their blood still pooling on the ground—
And then—the trembling motion of a lifted arm—
A hand that reaches out and beckons me.
The man who sighed!
I'm terrified but go to him and kneel where he lies
And take my flask and hold it to his lips.
The bloodied man takes pains to lift his head
But turns his face away and will not drink.
"Are any left alive?" he asks.
(The question helps to put my mind at ease,
That he should think about his comrades first.)
That done I lower them to his:
"I think you are the only one," I sigh.
He seems relieved to hear that grim report,
Which runs a shiver down my spine,

Then draws a deeper breath
And lets his eyes fall softly on the flask.

....

Standing in the belfry
Of a little country church,
Long ago deserted
And left here to fend for itself,
Which it has not done well.
Had to climb a wooden ladder
And put my faith in rungs (and legs)
No longer seeming sound enough to bear my weight,
And wriggle through a hole
Not more than shoulder width to get up here.
I should be careful where I stand,
But tell my feet they're on their own,
For I have fixed my eyes upon the Bell
Which yet hangs here
Silent in its iron yoke.
I stand and wonder it—
The thing it is,
The thing it used to be.
I put the palms of my hands on it.
"I can almost feel the sound of you," I say,
Then lift and tilt the Bell up toward me
And let it fall.
A bird startles from a tree!

I like to think there yet still stands
A little A-frame Cabin in the woods
Which I, with younger hands
And younger everything than I have now,
Erected there,
High on a densely wooded Hill,
Some forty years ago.
It almost broke my heart to part with it
And with the many Trees
That I had come to love
And think of as my own.
We belonged to each other I thought.
But I no longer had the strength and stamina
To keep the long way up to it—
A winding road of dirt and rock—
From washing out in heavy rains,
And finally did the only thing that I could do
And sold it to a younger neighbor friend of mine
Who owned the land adjoining it.
"I'll take good care of it," he said, "and of the trees,"
And I believed he would and hope he has.

I remember that last day—
Remember it often and with rue,
Standing there alone,
Already missing every thing my eyes could see,
When with a certainty I knew
The Cabin and the Trees were sad!
They were saying goodbye to me,
And they were sad.
I think they knew I'd never come back,

And I knew it too—
And we died in each other's arms that day.
I'm sure the Cabin and the Trees
Came back to life
Soon after my descending car got small
And disappeared around a leafy bend.

Life came more slowly back to me,
But did come back,
And something like my ghost
From time to time returns
And kindles up a fire in the stove
And steps outside and moves about
And stops and puts its arms around a Tree.
And if the solitary fox looks up some night
And sees a glow of Light play through the Cabin glass
When no one's there—
It's me.

....

Death is simply a returning
To the place it was always impossible to leave,
Becoming again what you had forgotten
That you always were.

....

When all were ordered to obey
He stood the ground and had his say,
And when they showed him to the door
He doffed his cap and walked away.

Basement.
Washing machine,
Cycle complete.
Wet rags and old towels.
Left overnight.
Remove midday next.
Something there in the bottom,
Dark against the white porcelain.
What is that?
Debris from a floor rag?—
Bend down to see a lifeless wasp!

Lift out.
Hold soft in the palm of my hand.
Examine.
All in a piece—
Hot water, detergent, vigorous agitation—
Not a single feature damaged!
Even fragile antennae intact!
How is that possible?
Then an antenna,
Ever so slightly,
Pulses a bit of motion!
Astonishment!!
A closer look—
Tiny tremors from a hind leg...
Energy from my palm, I think.
Post mortem stirrings.
Take it upstairs in my hand.
Sit and watch over it.
Hours pass.

Take it out in the garden air
To warm in the sun.
It stirs in the light.
Leave it there alone for awhile.
Return later.
Responds when taken up.

Back inside.
Still the wee signs of life...
More hours pass...
Night falls.
Still the tiny vital signs...

Bedtime.
Place on its underside.
Touch with my heart.
For first time
Wings slowly lift and spread!!
Like two arms held up,
As if in praise—
Or gratitude.
They stop and hold in place.
How strange!
Prolonged wonder.
Leave it there like that...

Morning comes.
Just as it was—
Wings still aloft.
No movement.
Surely she is gone.

Continued

Take her into my palm again.
A stirring!!
Brief flex of the body.
Then a slow closing of the wings,
Pulling in along her sides.

When gathered close—Stillness.
Turn her over on her back.
A little corpse,
Perfectly composed,
As if arranged.

Take her out.
Place her in a clump of spring chives—
Which will blossom soon.

....

I put my arms around a tree and hold it tight.
I enter it; it enters me.
I feel as if we two have made a singularity,
And it occurs to me that I'm as close to "God"
As I will ever will be.

....

I loved you at first sight, you know,
When first you caused my heart to soar,
And love you now no less than then
And will hereafter love you more.

In the beginning
There was yes and no,
Do and don't—
Expressions of approval,
Gruff corrections—
Which led to should and shouldn't,
And then to right and wrong;
And then alpha male man
Imagined alpha male "God,"
And right and wrong became good an evil,
And "no" and "shouldn't" became sin.
There was no good and evil.
Or sin and judgment—
In the beginning.

....

Twice now,
When I have gone out
To feed the birds,
I've come upon a sparrow
Disabled on the ground.
Both times I suffered helplessly.
Unable to pray,
All I could do was ache for it—and hope.
And both times,
When I returned at close of day
To see what had become of them
I could hardly bear
To turn my eyes that way.

Oh what deep, delicious sleep is this
That falls upon me now
And wraps me in a quilt of downy Light
And carries me away?
What sweet abduction, this!
Ahh! Forbid that I should ever wake again!
Oh, Great Mystery "God," Sleep on!

. . . .

A woman asks God:
　　"Do you love me?"
I understand you.
　　"But do you love me?"
I do not judge you.
　　"But do you love me?"
I have made you out of myself.
　　"Does that mean you love me?"
It means because I am—you are!
　　"But do you love me?"

God asks a woman:
　　Do you love me?
"I believe in you."
　　But do you love me?
"I pray to you."
　　But do you love me?
"I have made you out of my need for you."
　　Does that mean you love me?
"It means I am nothing without you.
　　But do you love me?

We all have Treasure buried in us,
Precious as a sleeping child's Dream,
And we should stake a claim,
And dig for it,
And it should be the purpose of our life
To discover that Treasure
And to Share it
And not to die
And have that Treasure buried twice.

....

When you can see Beauty
Even in ugly things
And Goodness
Even in things evil
And Meaning
Even in the senseless,
Then you have seen
The very face of God.

....

Ruthlessly Evolutionary,
Inexorable,
Utterly Indifferent,
Ferociously Beautiful,
Forever Before,
Ever After,
Always Now!

Church courtyard.
A large mound of shrubbery,
Dense and round-shouldered
And bending to the ground.
"What a neat hiding place for a kid!" I think,
And smile to myself...
Remembering...
As I walk by
And down the street
And out of sight,
I could not know
That under that great canopy of green,
Sheltered from the light of day
And from the sight
Of eyes that cannot see,
A woman lay unconscious,
An empty bottle of cheap wine
Held close to her,
As a little girl might hold close
A piece of satin cloth—
Or a rag doll.

....

I put my arms around a tree
And hold it tight,
My head turned to the side,
My cheek and ear
Pressed close to it.
To my astonishment I hear
A susurration
Coming from the tree!!

Or so it seems to me—
A steady din of sound,
As from a distant waterfall.
Maybe what I hear
Is just the background noise
The tree collects from here around
And whispers in my ear.
Or something seething
Deep beneath the ground.
Or maybe it's in me—
The susurration,
The distant waterfall—
The sound I hear
Coming from the tree.

....

I now take back my judgment
Of the Mighty Oak
That shaded out the life
Of countless acorn shoots,
(That struggled so to thrive,
Whose struggles were so short.)
And now the mammoth tree inspires me,
An acorn shoot
That struggled so for life,
Whose struggle was so long,
Whose life fulfills and justifies
The thousand little deaths
That happen in her shade.

December.
Early morning.
A long, dark hour yet
Before the break of day.
I step outside
And run into a wall of morning chill
Which braces me
And takes my breath away,
And when I lift my eyes
And see the clear, black Sky,
All Marveled as it is with Stars,
My heart and mind turn inside out!
And seeing me exposed like this,
The arms of that bright, sprawling Sky
Reach down and gather me
And lift me up
And hold me close,
And I can feel the pulsing heart of it,
And for a timeless moment
I no longer have a name—
And when I feel the earth beneath my feet again,
I drop my eyes,
Let loose a little cloud of breath,
And disappear into the dark,
All Marveled like the Sky.

....

I can feel proud,
But never worthy of praise;
I can feel remorse,
But never guilt.

"Pray for me," it says.
I stop and kneel down.
The small Japonica is failing.
It has not thrived for several years,
But now seems on the verge of giving up
And letting go.
(It shames me to admit how long it's been
Since first I noticed its decline
And only sighed and cast a feeble hope its way.)
This day I make the choice to intercede:
"I will pray for you, Japonica,"
I mutter loud enough for it to hear,
"The only way I know how"...

I soon return with garden tools
And push my shovel down and under it
And with one little heave
Lift up the cheerless plant
And place it on the ground nearby.
And after troweling loose the dirt inside
And round the hole,
And making fresh a bed of loam
(From potting mix I chance to have on hand),
I lift the failing plant again
And snug it back into its better place,
Then fill and press the gaps around
With more black soil from the bag
And smooth it level with the ground.
And after spreading down a quilt of hardwood mulch
And soaking it with water from the sky,
I get up from my knees.

A smallish pair of shiny black boots
Stand smartly side by side upon a step
Leading to the door of an old church,
Likely put there by a passerby who found them
Lying on the walk,
Or as an offering
From one who had no further use for them
And left them there,
Hoping they would find their way
Onto another little girl's feet.
They've been there now for three long weeks,
Lonely as a pair of little girl's boots
Sitting empty and unclaimed upon a step
Leading to the door of an old church.

....

I prayed for you, Japonica,
The only way that I knew how—
But it was not enough.
Had I but known how to pray
As others pray
You might be showing off
New shiny leaves this day
Instead of starking leafless there
All out of life.
But I don't think "God" works that way
Or has a say
When Desperation roots itself in plant—or man.
Your time was all used up, Japonica,
And though I tried
I could not change the Order of the Stars.

So all that's left for me to do
Is take you by the brittle stems
And with a little heave
Lift up what there remains of you
And take you where
Your "afterlife" begins.

[Oh, yes, it's true:
The human part of me
Breathes out a sigh
To leave you there
Atop the rubbish heap,
But not the better part.
The better part
Discards what's left of you
With all the blessed nonchalance
Of distant stars.]

....

The heart compassions
But does not convulse
To hear of an ancient woman,
Bent and blind,
And wracked with constant pain,
Who prays each night
That she will die in her sleep,
But how the heart excruciates
To hear of a young girl
Who each night
Makes the same prayer.

It was in a dream
That I,
A boy of only five ramshackle years,
Found myself walking in the Dark,
Lost and alone and trembling with fear...
When there appeared in that foreboding place
An eerie glow that seemed to beckon me,
And as I trembled toward it through the night,
I saw the light was coming from a great tree,
Vast and ghostly Bright,
And of an upward reach
Impossible to tell.
"Climb me," it whispered low,
And so,
Dismayed as I was,
I began to climb...
And was well up in the tree
When I looked down
And was terrified to find
How high it was I'd climbed.
And suddenly I was filled with fear
And froze in place,
My arms squeezed tight around
The tree of shimmering light,
Unable now to slide back down
Or shimmy up,
My cheek pressed close
Against the luminescent bark—
When just then
Beneath my cheek
I felt a small hole open in the tree

And heard a soft voice say:
"Do not be afraid,
But put close your eye,
To see what I will show."
And when I put my eye against the hole…
I saw at first nothing but the dark,
And then,
Slowly,
The light from a street lamp,
Casting a yellow glow
On quiet houses lined up side by side
Along a quiet street…
And then my eye zoomed up
To one such ordinary house,
Which surely was my own,
And to a window in an upper room
And through that window
To a bed
Where something lay all bundled up
Beneath a quilt,
Then to the face of a little boy
Who had been troubled by a fitful dream
But now lay sound asleep
Far way in a high place
Cradled in the soft arms of a hammock
Strung between two upper limbs
Of a vast and Luminous Tree.

A Tree:
It does not snicker, growl or glare
Nor can be said for anything to care.
It does not scoff or question why
Nor praise or blame,
Nor laugh or cry,
Just in a quiet, graceful way
Sends up its central arm,
And reaches high—
As far as rooted tree can reach—
Into the Sky,
Stretching for the Sun by day
And in the night—
For Stars!

....

You ask about
That shaky stand of bamboo poles
Back there behind the shed
Looking like a badly weathered Tepi shell.
Well, years ago
Small sprouts of bamboo
Found that ground
A hopeful place to stake a claim
And soon had enterprised themselves
Into a thriving density
Of tall and hardy shoots,
As straight as any gladiator's spear.
At first I welcomed and admired them,
As they were something of a novelty
Among the common growth back there

And reached impressive heights.
But soon I found it quite impossible
To keep my peace with them,
For they began to claim more land
Than I was willing to concede—
Your smile tells you know just what I mean—
And so at last declared a kind of war on them,
And after months of fighting hand to hand,
Mostly in the trenches underground,
I finally won the war.
I did take prisoners, though—
If you can call a thing you've killed a prisoner.
You see them there,
All huddled in that geometric form,
Still standing where they fell—
Oh Yes—the fountain. I'm sorry.
Sometimes I do go on.

....

In the little boy I was
You could not see
The man I would become
Nor can you see
In the man I have become
The little boy I was.
But we were both there then—
And both here now.

She keeps a small stone Buddha
On the stand beside her bed.
And every night she takes it in her hand
And holds it close,
As one holds close
A precious memory
Or a dream
Or the longing for an absent God.
And when the Stars come out inside of her
She sets it down
And gives herself to sleep.
The Buddha watches over her,
Placidly,
With eyes of polished stone.

....

When she writes
It's always with the little "i"
I think for her the little "i"
Denotes the Upper case.

....

When he asks what I think of the billions of animals
Being burned alive in Australia's raging fires in the Bush,
I answer that I do not think of them.
"You don't care?" he says with obvious dismay.
"As much as God," I say.
"You do care then?"
"I did not say that."
He looks at me in disbelief.

I look away.
"It's true. I do care,
Probably more than God.
I should have said I cannot think of them—
I'd risk my life
To rescue even one,
But cannot think of them."

....

A summer night.
A little girl sits alone
On a cement step
Peering into a glass jar
Which she holds nestled in her lap,
A piece of old screen
Serving as a lid.
She has been watching them
For quite some time,
The softly blinking yellow lights,
Vaguely wondering
Whether she's really thinking about them
Or thinking about herself.
Then she removes the lid,
Sets the jar in the grass,
And goes inside,
The screen door
Making a quiet banging sound behind her,
Which makes her turn and look.

"Do you really believe that!" he asks,
Looking at me in disbelief.
I smile, patiently.
"Do you really believe what you believe?" I ask him back.
"I do not question it," he says,
His words closing like a steel trap.
I smile again.
"We are different that way," I say.
"Though every Atom of my body
Approves of my belief,
Each night I fall asleep still Mystified
And wake each morning
Unable to rub the Wonder from my eyes."
It's his turn to smile now,
Which he does, patiently.

....

Went down to church tonight
To check the trap I'd set
To see if I had caught the squirrel
That somehow managed in
But couldn't manage out
(And was therefore already trapped)
And found inside the crafty apparatus
A little figure huddled there
All wrapped in tail,
Motionless as a lump of grey stone.
"Do not be afraid, I said;
"You are with a friend."
Carefully I lifted the trap
And carried it as smoothly up the stairs

As somewhat shaky arms and legs allowed
And out the door
And placed it in the grass,
Then lifted up the steel grate,
That only an hour or two before
Slammed down and shut him in,
And let the frightened little fellow out.
A blur of streaking grey and he was gone!
I had set the captive free—
Of both his traps—
And we shared an Exultation!

. . . .

One Atom asks of another:
"Who are we? And where?
And what are we doing here?"
The other Atom scratches his head,
And together they puzzle such questions
Until they are old and grey,
And it never occurs to them
That they are actually hard at work,
Doing their very small part
To fortify a tender shoot of grass
Which is fighting for its life
In a field dense with grass,
On a Planet
Whirling round a Star,
The Star lost in a great Swirl of Stars,
The great Swirl itself
Lost in a Wonderland
Of Time and Space.

The old Maple tree was taken down today—
As everything old is finally taken down—
And when the night
Has fallen round the open space
Where only hours ago it stood,
I make my way to it,
And take the little step it is
To lift myself up on the flat remains,
And for some spell of time
Stand silent there and let a Stillness
Settle over me.
I close my eyes, remembering,
Then lift my arms
And let the branches of my heart
Reach up and out into the blackened sky,
And let my feet take root
In wood still fresh and fragrant under me,
And for some little while,
And for a final time,
The Maple is alive again!
Until the dark but smiling figure standing there
Steps down
And turns for home.

....

Magic—without a Magician!

A fire burns until it starves—
Candles, Forests, Hearts, and Stars—
And writers write
Until there's nothing left to burn.

....

I stand here all alone with him
Beneath this cloudy shower of marble dust
That has,
At this late hour of the day,
All but covered me from head to toe,
And lift my eyes to him,
This lovely and colossal shepherd boy
Who towers over me,
And Wonder him...
"I've let you out of stone," I say—
"And out of me."
And then step back and lift my hands
And look at them,
These living things all calloused as they are
And covered as they are with marble residue,
And Wonder them...
I take my apron off
And place it on the bench where now I sit,
Then drop my head
And sob into my hands.

The squirrel is back,
Attending church again,
Same fix as before—
Alone and boxed in,
This time closed in an upper room
Hiding behind a bank of filing cabinets,
As far into the corner place as he can go.
Again I set the trap,
Crunchy peanut butter on a cracker square.
Before I leave the room
I hear a sound back there,
A faintly uttered sound.
And I go and get a cup of water
And set it the floor
Beside the steel cage.
"Please take and drink," I say.
I wonder if you can understand—
The faintly uttered sound I heard
Coming from that dark corner place
Was a feeble little voice
That barely managed out:
"I thirst."

....

The warbled serenade of the wren
This early morning hour
Wriggles through me
Like a silver thread
Pulled by some enchanted spirit
From another realm.

Last night in a dream
I found myself in Jacob's skin
And on the ground
Tangled in a fierce struggle
With a Dark Presence.
Though fastened in its grasp,
I did not fear,
And refused to give way,
And fought on through the night,
Until at last
The fight went out of the Dark Presence,
And I felt its hand rest soft on my head,
And I rose from the ground,
As from the dead,
And the Sun fell upon me.

Acknowledgments

It was a pleasure working with all the people at Columbus Publishing Lab: Quentin Russell, an acquisition editor who impressed me with his careful reading of and commentary on my bulky submission; Heather Shaw, who did the lengthy transcription; Doug Davis, who spent long hours formatting the pages and who designed such a thoughtful and evocative cover; and Emily Hitchcock, the Chief Executive of CPL, who stepped in to manage the project during a difficult time, and was involved in every aspect of the production. She was patient and supportive throughout, and in times of stress and indecision, hers was the cheerful voice that I could always depend on to calm and encourage. I can't thank her enough.

All proceeds from the sale of this book will be donated by the author to the following charitable organizations:

Sheldrick Wildlife Trust (founded in 1977 by David Sheldrick)

Dian Fossey Gorilla Fund (initiated as Karisoke in 1969)

Rainforest Trust (officially incorporated on Dec. 8, 1988)